I'M RIGHT. YOU'RE WRONG. NOW WHAT?

How to Break Through Any Relationship Stalemate Without Fighting, Folding or Fleeing

JacLynn Morris, M.Ed. & Paul L. Fair, Ph.D.

SOURCEBOOKS, INC.
NAPERVILLE, ILLINOIS

This publication is designed to provide accurate and authoritative information in regard to the subject matter covered. It is sold with the understanding that the publisher is not engaged in rendering legal, accounting, or other professional service. If legal advice or other expert assistance is required, the services of a competent professional person should be sought.—*From a Declaration of Principles Jointly Adopted by a Committee of the American Bar Association and a Committee of Publishers and Associations*
Published by Sourcebooks, Inc.

P.O. Box 4410, Naperville, Illinois 60567-4410
(630) 961-3900
FAX: (630) 961-2168
www.sourcebooks.com

Morris, JacLynn, 1950-
  I'm right. You're wrong. Now what? : how to break through any relationship stalemate / JacLynn Morris and Paul L. Fair.
    p. cm.
  Includes index.
  ISBN 1-4022-0179-6 (alk. paper)
  1. Man-woman relationships. I. Fair, Paul L., 1944- II. Title.
HQ801 .M778 2004
306.7—dc22

                           2003026307

Printed and bound in the United States of America
VP   10   9   8   7   6   5   4   3   2   1

This book can help you solve two kinds of couples' problems:
The kind your partner will help you with and the kind your partner won't.

Contents

Acknowledgments

We are deeply grateful to dozens of men and women whose names you will not find here. Some of these people came to our workshops. Some participated in therapy groups. Others we met and talked with at our favorite coffee shop. All of them entrusted us with their personal stories and, with wonderful generosity, granted us permission to share their experiences with you. Without them this book would not exist.

We also want to thank the two extraordinary people who encouraged, advised, loved, cooked for, and put up with us as we worked on this book. We're lucky they married us: JacLynn's husband, Bruce H. Morris—and Paul's wife, Virginia R. Cueto

And we wish to thank our respective children—the best and brightest fans anyone could ever have:

Emily and Peter Morris, JacLynn and Bruce's children

Alexandra Cueto, Paul and Virginia's daughter

There are many others we wish to thank for sharing their insights and helping us to make this a better book. Some touched our lives years ago and in doing so helped put us on the path that led to this book. Others showed us new ways to make relationships work wonderfully well. Some gave us valuable feedback about our approach. Several read and reread countless drafts. And in one way or another, each of them helped us hang in there when the going got tough:

Elizabeth Arnold
Sheri Ashworth
Bart Bakaley
Dennis A. Bagarozzi, Ph.D.
Candy and Steve Berman
The Beckwiths: Aaron, Amy, Beverly, Bruce, and Henri Simoneti; Carl, Claudia and Bill Ferguson; David, Edward, Ellen, Gary, George, Iris, Jane, Jason, Jenna, Jessica, Jodi and Stefan Cohen; Judy, Kent, Linda, Mildred, and Wendy

Iris Bolton, Ph.D.

Marsha Boyes, R.N.

Patty and Larry Brown

Lisa and Bob Citronberg

Glen Colton

Mary Crossman

Aimee Daly

Carrell A. Dammann, Ph.D.

Margaret Danzig

Bert Devorsetz

Steve Douglas

Denise, Eddie, and Hanna Esserman

Carol Faas

Mary Ann Fair

Nancy and Wayne Freedman

JoAnne and Stuart Finestone

Bob Finger

Kathy Foreman

Viki Freeman (and her mother, Millie West)

Gloria Frisch

Roni Funk, MSW

Mickey Goodman

Gail and Allen Gordon

Sherry Haber

A. Neil Harrison, M.D.

Debbie Harrison

Leah and Mark Harrison

Sharon and Robert Harrison

Tom Harrison

Joanna Haynes-Lahr

Carolyn Hessel

Steve Hightower

Harlyn and Maurice Joseph

Melissa and Mark Kadish

Ethel and Ted Kopkin

Al Kitchen

Nancy and Steve Landesberg

Harriet and Henry Leibowitz

Charla and Steve Lerman

Phyllis and Ira London

Eileen and Ralph Levy

Wendy Lipshutz, MSW

Amy Lively

Michael Mandel

Roddrick Mayberry and the staff at Starbuck's Store #978

Anita M. Morris

Barbara and Harvey Mays

Amy Sue Maziar

Patty and Howard Maziar, M.D.

Maggie Okun

Caryl and Bobby Paller

Lorie Penniman

Jean and Marc Pickard

Shirley Retter

Frank J. Rizzo

Frank Rizzo, Jr.

Steve Ross

Leslie and Tod Rubin, M.D.

Denise Sanders

Dr. Carol Samuels

Margaret (Peggy) and Ken Saxon

Jay Slotnick

Diane Sollee

George Stern

Linda Stone
Michael Treadwell
Hope and Ed Tudanger
Linda Bressler Wand
Phyllis and Michael Weiser
Sheryl Westerman
Ava Wilensky, Ph.D.

We are especially grateful to these authors for their willingness to advise and their capacity to empathize:

Melissa Faye Green; Terry Kay; Rochelle Krich; Harold S. Kushner; Harriet Lerner, Ph.D.; Michael Lucker; Liza Nelson; Robyn Freedman Spizman; and Nick Taylor

Thanks also to Jack Perry and the enthusiastic staff at Sourcebooks, including:

Christine Garcia
Jenna Jakubowski
Laura Kuhn
Todd Stocke
Sarah Tucker

And finally, we want to thank those who believed in our book before it was one and who applied their considerable skills to bring this project to life:

Hillel Black, our editor
Bob DiForio, our agent
Sharon Kraun, our public-relations wizard

Introduction:
There's Just Got to Be a Better Way

Beyond fighting, folding, or fleeing

Fifteen hours a week, forty-six weeks a year, we meet at a coffee shop in Atlanta, Georgia, where we drink gallons of coffee, pace, argue, scribble, swap stories, butt heads, and write books. This is our second book. Our first one, *From Me to You: The Reluctant Writer's Guide to Powerful, Personal Messages,* took us nearly three years to finish. There were plenty of reasons that it took us so long.

Our writing styles and work habits are miles apart. Our expectations seldom match. We come from different religious backgrounds. One of us loves to be right. The other one hates to be wrong. And both of us can be very stubborn.

Still, we like and respect each other, which is why, over the years, we've tried to lessen the strains between us by drawing on every single conflict resolution, negotiation, compromise, communication, and assertiveness skill that we know. And when that hasn't worked, we've resorted to talking to one another in those soft, overly careful phrases that therapists learn to use. (A natural choice since one of us is a therapist-turned- writer and the other a clinical psychologist.) Even so, there were times when just about the only thing we could agree on was how glad we were that we weren't married to each other.

Joking about that one afternoon, we found ourselves in a lengthy discussion about how we handle our disagreements. And as we talked on, we admitted that many of the same issues and personal quirks that complicate our disputes with one another also come into play in what for us is the most significant and valued part of our lives—our marriages.

Wishing we knew a better (and quicker) way to get through the inevitable disputes that crop up in a marriage, we wondered, *Are there direct steps that partners with strong differences of opinion, style, personality, judgment, and belief can take to keep moving forward together when they find themselves at odds?* Can they do that without one person trying to change the other? What if one of the two people won't cooperate? Could we come up with an easy-to-follow, effective problem-solving model that would help one person in the relationship begin to calmly address and resolve a dispute anyway? Could the same problem-solving model be used whether couples are dealing with a small skirmish or are caught up in something that feels more like a full-scale war?

Looking for answers led us to write this book. And that's where the built-in benefits of being "coffee-shop writers" afforded us a wonderful advantage. Day after day at the coffee shop, we get to spend time with a remarkably diverse group of men and women who have taken an ongoing interest in our work. So we began our work on this project by asking our coffee-shop "friends" about the kinds of disputes they have with their spouses. Most of them raised their eyes toward the heavens and immediately launched into tales of their own "I'm Right/You're Wrong" marital moments.

Sometimes they spoke of encounters filled with blunders, hurt feelings, and dead ends. Other times they smiled and described experiences in which they'd moved calmly through irritations, arguments, major misunderstandings, and feuds with their spouses. Those stories in particular struck us as fascinating and strangely comforting. Simply knowing that warring spouses armed with goodwill found ways past their conflicts strengthened our faith in the possibilities.

Early on, we noticed that as different as these people were from one another, when they were successful at getting beyond their disputes, they all had something important in common. Instead of staying stuck in their first, understandably negative reactions to a conflict, the people whose stories found their way into this book turned their thoughts away from *who* was right or wrong and moved on to consider *what* they could do to improve things. It's as if they were asking, "Now what?"

These people did something that many of us—especially in the heat of the moment—don't think about or even know we can do! They asked themselves the kinds of questions that calmed their thoughts and feelings, freed their energy, and unblocked their creativity so that they could begin to cast about looking for ways past their relationship roadblocks.

Even when they were feeling attacked, blamed, angry, or fearful, their minds raced ahead, asking questions that prompted them to look for ways to get unstuck. Recognizing that certain questions can propel people beyond their preoccupation with who is right and who is wrong, we set out to find a handful of simply-worded, powerful questions that could guide us—and you too—calmly through an "I'm Right/You're Wrong" conflict.

After many months and with help from our families, friends, clients, professional associates, and fellow coffee-shop regulars, we developed six questions that really work. From there, we watched the men and women we met in our workshops, coffee shops, and therapy groups use their answers to the six questions to work through a host of common couples' conflicts.

With wonderful generosity, the people we met along the way agreed to try our ideas, help us fine-tune our approach, and recount their experiences for you here. Those whose stories you are about to read preferred to share their thoughts and feelings anonymously, and we have honored their request by using fictional names. As you read along, you will see how they managed to summon the best of themselves and their partners even as the demands and intrusions of living intimately threatened to pull them apart.

When we started this project, both of us believed that there really are some couples' conflicts that can not be resolved. We still believe that. But we also thought that the alternative to conflict resolution was at best a temporary, uneasy peace and at worst a parting of the ways. Now we know better.

Now we know that if only one partner asks and writes out his or her answers to the six basic questions, the nature of their dispute is altered and improved in ways that are at once personal, direct, affectionate, effective, wise, and occasionally very funny. And we also know that answering the six questions helps people whose conflicts cannot be resolved to accept what is true, marshal their own resources, and come up with a solid back-up plan that leads to a satisfying conclusion anyway.

Sprinkled throughout this book are tales about and solutions to a wide range of couples' disagreements. These include quarrels about annoying personal habits, interfering in-laws, financial pressures, religious differences, selfish behaviors, a lack of intimacy, jealousy, addictions, inconsistent parenting styles, infidelity, and more.*

Watching people work through their clashes (blunders and all) and then take positive, realistic steps that lead to satisfying results taught us the value of asking ourselves questions. Showing us *which* questions to ask is the gift they gave us. And just as they gave it to us, we hope we are able to give it to you.

*This book does not address the needs of those whose partners are physically, sexually, or emotionally abusive. If you are in an unsafe relationship, we strongly encourage you to seek help. For a referral to an experienced therapist, support group, or "safe house" in your community, contact your local United Way office.

1

First Steps after the Last Straw

One day two people did the same old thing
but one of them did it differently

This is a book about a direct and effective way to settle your disputes without fighting, folding, or fleeing. By using the approach laid out for you here, you can make your way calmly past a host of "I'm Right/You're Wrong" couples' conflicts. *Even if your partner will not cooperate, you can use this problem-solving model on your own* to improve the tone of your disagreement, sort out what you want or need most from your partner, and come up with two practical action plans that lead to a satisfactory outcome.

The approach we are about to take you through begins with your written responses to these six questions:

1) What are my negative feelings?
2) What's the fairest way to describe the problem?
3) Why do I want to work things out?
4) How would I like things between us to be?
5) How can I actually get that?
6) And if that doesn't work, what else can I do?

To demonstrate how these questions can guide you safely through the stuck point in a conflict, Judith, a woman in her late thirties, agreed to let us show you what happened when she applied her answers to settle an ongoing dispute with her husband, Steve, about where, when, and how to air their differences.

Here is Judith's description of what she calls "the last straw":

"Last night everyone got home late. It was after nine o'clock before Steve and the kids and I sat down for dinner and by then all four of us were cranky. Naturally, the second we sat down, our daughter, Susan, started spouting off about how unfeeling I was, what a rotten mother I was. On and on she went.

"The whole time I was squirming inside, waiting for Steve to step in and tell her to stop—only he didn't. Susan's voice was getting louder and louder until I couldn't take it anymore. I looked up at her and hissed, 'Susan, cut it out!' But she just glared at me and started picking on her twin brother, Andrew.

"When I told her to leave Andrew alone, she started in on me again. She accused me of always running away instead of facing her and hearing her out. I gave Steve one of those why-don't-you-speak-up-for-me looks. Instead, he leaned over, took Susan's hand and thundered, 'She's absolutely right! Why don't you answer her already? What kind of a mother are you?'

"That's when something inside me snapped. I couldn't believe he'd done that! As parents we're supposed to stick together. That's huge for me and he knew it! I shot up out of my chair, stormed into our bedroom, and waited for Steve. When he finally came in, he held up his hand and said, 'I don't want to talk about this!'

"'Well we're going to!' I told him.

"'No, no we're not,' he said. Then he turned his back to me and walked out of the room. I was boiling mad. That was the last straw! I grabbed my car keys, marched past him, slammed the door behind me, and choking back my tears, drove to the shopping mall near our home. I'd never done anything like that before.

"When I got to the mall, the stores were closed and the parking lot was almost empty. I parked under a light, saw a guard sitting in a white security van, walked over to him, and said, 'I'm an angry, angry woman who's just had a huge fight with her husband. I need a place to blow off steam and I'm going to sit in my car right over there and holler for a while, but I want to be safe. So, keep an eye on me, OK?' He looked at me like I was crazy, but he shrugged and said he would.

Then I walked back to the car, climbed in, locked the doors, and shrieked and sobbed and yelled. Huge waves of frustration, rage, and hurt blew out of me. Every fight we'd had since the kids were born flashed through my mind, but it only took me about three minutes to scream it all out. After that, I just sat there thinking.

"I thought about how many times Steve and I had gone round and round on this exact same thing. How many times I'd listened to his excuses, explanations, and apologies. And how many times he'd agreed that as parents we should back each other up. Every one of those times I had agreed to forgive and forget. And things would get better for a little while. But sooner or later we ended up right back in the same place. The more I remembered, the angrier I got. I was so fed up that all I could think was, 'I want out!'

"In that moment, I didn't care about my marriage. I didn't have the energy or the desire to keep trying to fix things. The words in my head were, 'I am only in this relationship as long as I want to be and not a minute longer!' All of a sudden I was getting myself back and I liked that. And then I got amazingly calm. I realized I really could get myself out of this marriage. Just knowing that made me feel better, stronger, and calmer.

"By then, it was so late and I was so cold sitting in that car that I wanted to go home. I didn't want to be in charge of fixing the things that were wrong between us any more. All I wanted was to hold on to the knowledge that I really could leave my marriage. So I held on to that thought as if my life depended on it and drove home. The house was dark. Thankfully, everyone was asleep. No one noticed that I sat up in a chair all night. I left the house this morning before Steve woke up. I'm still so angry I can't stand to be in the same room with him!"

When Judith finished speaking, her eyes were filled with tears.

Since Judith frequented the coffee shop often, she was familiar with our work on this book. We asked her if she wanted to go through the six basic questions with us. She said she'd give it a try. Then she took a few deep breaths, blew her nose, wrapped her arms around herself, and settled back in her chair.

Minutes later, we handed her a printed sheet of paper that had the same six questions on it that we listed at the beginning of this chapter. Then, we plugged in a tape recorder and captured her answers. As you follow her words, you'll notice that when Judith seemed to get hung up on a particular question, we made some suggestions to help her along.

Question 1: What are my negative feelings?

"You want me to list my negative feelings? Fine! I'm *furious*! What Steve did last night was wrong on every single level. Susan did what kids do; she tried to play one parent against the other. That I can deal with. What I can't handle is being married to someone who sides with the kids against me, *humiliates* me in front of them, and who now won't even talk to me about what he's done! And I'm *hurt* that Steve didn't even ask me if something had happened earlier in the day that might have led up to Susan's behavior. He just took her side without a second thought.

"I'm *mortified* that Steve blasted me in front of the kids. I'm *exhausted* because I haven't slept. And no matter what Steve says now, I'm *afraid* to trust that he's ever going to change. And I'm *sick* of having this kind of thing happen over and over."

Judith's tears stopped. She hugged herself, slouched back in her chair without speaking for several minutes, and then she said she was ready to continue.

Question 2: What's the fairest way to describe the problem?

"You've got to be kidding! There's nothing even slightly fair about any of this! Try answering anyway? All right. The problem is that Steve and I disagree big-time about when, where, and how husbands and wives should argue. I think arguments between a husband and wife should happen in private. I think neither one of us should ever do something that embarrasses the other—especially in front of the kids. Steve says he agrees, but obviously his actions say something else!

"And we also disagree about the right way to respond to our kids. Steve thinks we should immediately respond to any and all requests our kids make. I think that parents need to talk things over between themselves first and then decide how to handle the kinds of complicated requests that kids make these days."

When she finished speaking, Judith sat up in her chair and uncrossed her arms for the first time.

Question 3: Why do I want to work things out?

"Who says I want to do that? Oh, you mean, can I think of any reasons why it might be a good idea to work this out once and for all?"

Judith said nothing for several minutes. She seemed deep in thought. Then she began talking very softly.

"I don't want my children to grow up with parents who are always fighting. And I know Steve doesn't want that either. His parents used to be at each other's throats all the time, and Steve has told me how hard that was on him.

"It would be good to work things out because it would be nice to get back to being a family that enjoys each other. I remember a trip we took to the beach once, where the four of us collected so many seashells that Steve had to rush out to a luggage store and buy an extra suitcase so we could bring them all home. We barely made it to the airport on time to get our plane. But Steve never complained. And I remember when the twins were little and so cute in their Halloween costumes, Steve would wait patiently at the top of every street to be sure our two goblins were safe.

"Steve does nice things for me, too. In fact, last week he made a whole pot of chili for me because he knows how much I love his secret recipe.

"So, yeah, I can find a lot of good reasons to hang in here and stay married. But I'm still not ready to make up my mind one way or the other!"

Question 4: How would I like things between us to be?

"Well it's no longer just a question of what I want in this one instance. I mean, Steve can't very well undo what he did last night, can he? So now I need to really think about where we go from here and about the bigger wants I have— like what I'd like from Steve as a husband and a coparent. That's a lot harder to figure out. My thoughts are so jumbled that I'd do better trying to write down what I'd like."

Judith reached into her handbag and pulled out a memo pad and pencil. Then she jotted down a few things, tore up the paper, and started in on another one. A few minutes later, she handed her paper to us. This is what she wrote:

How I'd like things to be:

1. When it comes to dealing with the kids, I'd like the two of us to present a unified front.
2. When there's a problem, I'd like us to talk about things as soon as they come up.
3. I'd like us to stop arguing in front of the kids.

When we finished reading her note, Judith told us:

"I think this is the first time in years that I've gotten clear about what I'd like. In the past, every time we've run into this problem, I'd get all caught up in the details of the event—as if it was some kind of stand-alone issue. Then I'd get so angry that I'd press Steve to explain himself—and that never worked!

"But this time, it doesn't matter to me why we keep having the same fight over and over again. I just want the three things that I wrote down on that piece of paper. That's it. I want those things, period."

Question 5: How can I actually get that?

"You mean, how can I get Steve to give me the three things I want? I'd be happy if I could get Steve to give me even one of those things. Which of the three do I want the most? For starters, how about finding a way to stop fighting in front of the kids? I don't know what it's going to take to get that, but that's where I'd like to start. Then, I want us to stand together when the kids ask for permission to do things. And I want Steve to promise me that we'll talk about our arguments privately.

"But I don't even know how to get Steve to see that this isn't about what happened at dinner last night. It's about how we treat each other as husband and wife and how we cooperate as parents. Look, the only way I could get what I want is to ask Steve straight out. But if I did that, I'd probably start crying before I got the first words out of my mouth. Then he'd think this is just me being overly emotional. I already know from past experience that if we sit down to talk about this that's exactly what will happen.

"You're suggesting I picture myself telling Steve that, even if I do cry, I want him to take me seriously? Um, I've never done that. Well, I guess if I started crying I could take a deep breath like I do when the kids are driving me crazy. Then before Steve had a chance to say a single word I could just keep on going like I'm talking to myself. Maybe say something like, 'Steve, even though I'm very emotional about this I want you to pay attention to what I'm saying. This is important to me. We both want to be good parents and we both know that the kids try to play us off against each other. We keep saying we have to stand together, so now I want the two of us to come up with a definite plan to make sure that we do. I want you to sit here and be calm and for both of us to stay here until we can come up with two ideas we both like.'

"Would that help me get what I want? Maybe. At least it might get us thinking about solving things instead of blaming each other for this mess."

Question 6: And if that doesn't work, what else can I do?

"Well, if Steve doesn't get that this problem isn't going to be magically solved just because he apologizes, I guess I could tell him I'm thinking of calling it quits.

"What about something less extreme? Maybe show him my note about the three things I want? But I don't think that's a good idea. Steve might turn the fact that I wrote to myself into some sort of joke and that would make things worse.

"Could I tell Steve how I want him to react before I showed him what I wrote? Uh, I think that's weird but I guess I could do it by saying something like, 'Steve, this morning I was thinking about the problems that keep showing up between us, and I was trying to figure out what I really wanted from you. I came up with three things that I wrote down on a piece of paper. And I'd like to show you this paper, but I don't want you to laugh at me or poke fun at me either because that will make me feel really foolish. Agreed?' I don't like the idea of showing him my note, but I suppose I will if I have to."

After that, Judith looked at her watch and said she had to head home and get some sleep before the kids and Steve got home. She told us she still wasn't sure what she was going to do, but said she felt a little better and assured us that she'd let us know what happened. Three and a half weeks later, she filled us in.

Outcome

"The day I ran into the two of you and spilled my guts about our fight, Steve and I barely spoke 'til after eleven o'clock at night when the kids went to bed.

Steve broke the silence when he asked me if I was still mad at him. I didn't know what to say, so I didn't answer. Then he acted all pitiful and wailed, 'I've already apologized. What more do you want?'

"I sputtered, 'What do I want? I don't want your damn apologies. I just want this to stop happening, that's what!'

"'You want what to stop?' he demanded.

"I looked at him like, what kind of an idiot are you? And I was thinking, 'What do you mean 'what'?' But I caught myself because I didn't want to make things worse. And that's when I remembered the note I wrote. Can you believe I pulled that paper out of my pocketbook and handed it to him without a word?

"Steve definitely looked surprised. But he sat down and read it. And you know the weirdest thing? When I handed him that note (instead of doing what I normally do, which is to fight back or try to force him to explain why he'd behaved so miserably toward me) that's when he started talking! Steve talked about his childhood experiences with more feeling than he'd ever shared with me. And for the first time, I saw how his upbringing had shaped the way he acted as a husband and a father.

"Then Steve told me other things that explained why he was so clueless about how fathers and mothers don't have to be played off against each other. He talked for a long time and I just listened. When he said he thought parents should be able to disagree about their kids, I told him I thought so too—but not in front of them! Then I told him some things he didn't know about what had happened to me growing up.

"Talking about our backgrounds was a big deal because it changed the way we saw each other. It was like now we understood more about why each of us does the things we do. So we were both feeling better about each other. But I still kept thinking, 'Can I really trust him to argue with me in private and then stand with me in the face of pressure from our children?'

"I decided to say that out loud to Steve. When I did, he reached for my hand and he looked sad. He told me that for the very first time he really understood how much it hurt me when he challenged me in front of the kids.

"'From now on,' he announced, 'I'll try to just catch myself and stop arguing with you in front of them. I promise.'

"'Yeah but what if you don't, then what?' I asked him.

"He said, 'Well…how about this? You could just touch my arm and tap your fingers for a second. I'll know what that means and I'll stop.'

"Steve even suggested that we give this problem of ours a name. He said why not call it the 'NIP thing,' which stands for 'Not in Public!'

"Has the problem gone away? There are times when the same thing still happens. Not as often, but it happens. Only, now that I know more about what's going on behind the scenes with him, I don't take things as personally as I used to. And Steve really does try to catch himself quickly. But if he screws up, I just say something quiet about the 'NIP thing' and that works pretty well!

"And another thing that's different is that now when I want to talk about things with Steve, he doesn't just turn around and walk out of the room; he stays there with me. And the best part is that the kids are starting to realize they can't play us off against each other like they used to.

"Were the questions helpful to me? Yes, especially the last three. (*How would I like things between us to be? How can I actually get that? And if that doesn't work, what else can I do?*) My answers to those gave me the first sense of hope I'd ever had about my ability to do something to make things better without waiting for Steve to make the first move. Plus answering those questions made it easier to figure out what I really wanted from Steve instead of staying stuck in the details of the argument like I always used to. Once I knew exactly what I'd like, the next questions helped me stop worrying about how Steve would react when I told him what I wanted.

"And the last question, the one that says, 'What else can I do?' Well, answering that one helped me get ready to tell Steve that I wanted him to listen to me and take me seriously. I realize Steve did that without me even asking—but it helped me a lot to know what I'd do if he didn't.

"Even though I didn't end up doing things the way I rehearsed them with you, answering your questions pumped up my courage so much that I even surprised myself when I handed Steve the note I'd written. Altogether, I think answering the questions left me feeling hopeful instead of fuming mad. And that was a first!"

WHERE DO YOU GO FROM HERE?

At this point, you've seen how asking and answering six basic questions helped Judith work through a hurtful, ongoing dispute with her husband. So you may be tempted to move on to the chapters that deal with the kinds of conflicts or disagreements that you face in your own life. *But we strongly recommend that you read the next chapter before you get underway.*

Chapter Two, which follows one man's tale of marital discord, shows you how to get the most from your personal answers to each question, gives you an easy way to handle your distracting thoughts and worries as they come to mind, helps you initiate a calm discussion with your partner, and prepares you to hang in there when the going gets tough.

2

Getting Unstuck without Coming Unglued

Answering six questions to get what you want (or need) from your partner

Shortly after we started working on this book, we were asked to speak to a small group of people about couples and conflict. We had already begun our presentation when a harried-looking, fifty-something man arrived. He picked up our handout materials and leafed through them distractedly. Then he took a seat at the back of the room and sat there shaking his head as though he disagreed with everything we said. After about ten minutes of this, apparently unable to hold back any longer, the man raised his hand insistently and challenged us:

"Look, I'm head of my company's human-resources department. I came here hoping to learn something new about conflict resolution. Well, I've been listening to you talk about your approach to couples and conflict and while it seems logical enough, it just isn't going to work—at least not for an old-fashioned, long-time married man like me.

"I'm from the John Wayne generation. Men like me don't talk to their wives about our worries or our feelings. We keep those things to ourselves," he insisted. "And while there are things I'd like my wife to do differently, if you think that me asking myself a handful of questions will make that happen, then you just don't know my wife," he told us earnestly.

Hearing that, everyone burst out laughing. When the room quieted, we smiled and asked this man, whom we'll call "Scott," if he could give us an example of something he'd like his wife to do differently.

Scott nodded and said, "At work lately, I'm having trouble helping people solve their problems. It's like I've lost my professional edge or something.

Anyway, by the end of the day I feel so down in the mouth that all I can think is, 'I'm lousy at my job,' and, 'Nothing I do helps anybody.'"

Waving his hands back and forth in the air as if he hoped to erase the words he'd just spoken, Scott continued, "Look, you don't need to know about my troubles at work. I'm just telling you this so you'll understand what I mean when I say that my wife is not a very nurturing person, and there's no way I'm going to be able to change that about her.

"Here's an example. Every day for the past six weeks, I go home after work and walk in the door with my shoulders all slumped over just hoping that my wife will give me a concerned look, a pat on the shoulder—any kind of comfort. But she never does. Not once in the thirty-four years that we've been married! Is it too much for me to ask her to be a little bit sympathetic and offer me some comfort?"

We assured Scott that what he wanted didn't strike us as too much to ask for.

"What happens when you ask your wife to comfort you?" we asked.

"What do you mean *what* happens when I ask her to comfort me? I don't ask her to do that! I'm not about to tell her I'm feeling insecure about myself. I told you, men like me don't do that sort of thing with their wives.

"Besides, I shouldn't have to ask my wife for something so obvious. When I come home looking completely worn down and worried, how hard is it to figure out that I've had a rotten day? All she has to do is treat me the same way that I treat her whenever she feels down.

"When my wife's upset, I'm wonderful to her! Either I cheer her up by getting her to laugh or I give her a big hug and tell her everything's going to be okay. Of course, if it's really a big thing, I remind her that whatever the problem is, I'm ready and willing to help her.

"But when *I'm* feeling really down, my wife acts like she doesn't even notice I'm upset! She just starts talking about what *her* day was like without even asking me about mine. It's unfair and I'm sick of it!"

"Scott, if you knew an easy way to get comfort from your wife, would you try it?" we asked.

"Depends. I'm not going into some long-winded, touchy-feely conversation or into couple's therapy with her. I already told you that I am not the kind of man who talks about my deep needs or things like that."

"Fair enough," we told him. "But if you knew how to get comforted by your wife without having what you call a 'touchy-feely conversation,' and if you could do that like John Wayne might have, would you want to try it?"

"Of course," he said, "but short of running around the house saying John Wayne things to my wife like, 'little lady, I don't take kindly to your attitude'— I don't think that's going to happen."

Smiling in appreciation of Scott's John Wayne rendition, we pressed on and asked if he'd be willing to answer each of the basic questions out loud to see where it led, just as an experiment. "And to help you get the most from each of your answers, we'll coach you along the way," we added.

Scott thought about it for a moment, shrugged, and said, "Sure, why not?"

GETTING THE MOST FROM YOUR PERSONAL ANSWERS

Because we were in a workshop setting, we wrote the six questions down along the left side of the blackboard at the front of the room. To the right of the questions, we left space for Scott's answers. Then we added another column for Scott to track any distracting thoughts or worries that might pop up along the way. We explained that when people sit down to write out their answers to the basic questions, it's normal for random, irrelevant, jumbled, unkind, unpleasant, or contradictory thoughts and worries to come to mind.

The trouble is that these thoughts and worries can take you off track or make it difficult to answer one or more questions. And unless you do something with them (like drop them into the margin) those swift-moving, distracting thoughts can plunge you right back into a host of negative reactions or cloud your mind with unrelated, nonproductive thoughts. So *as you ask and answer each of the six questions, it's especially helpful to notice and then jot down in the right hand margin every single distracting thought or worry that occurs to you*. Nothing that comes to mind is off limits.

Now go ahead and take a look at the chart below. We wrote this out on the blackboard at the front of the room before we began working with Scott. This is the format that we recommend you use when you are ready to create your own written responses to the six basic questions.

Basic Questions:	Answers:	Distracting Thoughts and Worries:
1. What are my negative feelings?		
2. What's the fairest way to describe the problem?		
3. Why do I want to work things out?		
4. How would I like things between us to be?		
5. How can I actually get that?		
6. And if that doesn't work, what else can I do?		

As you read Scott's answers to each question, we'd like you to notice how much more thoughtful and meaningful his responses became when we told him what each question is designed to do, gave him coaching cues to help him get the most from his answers, and encouraged him to voice his distracting thoughts and worries along the way (in order for us to drop them into the margin for him).

Question 1:	Scott's Initial Answer:	Distracting Thoughts and Worries:
What are my negative feelings?	What do you think I'm feeling? I'm **annoyed** at Liz. When I'm down, why can't she comfort me? She makes me so **angry**. Maybe I shouldn't be **mad** at her because she does a lot of good things. I'm starting to **resent** the time I spend whining about something as little as this is. By the way, I think this experiment is absurd!	

When we'd finished writing out what Scott had said, he grinned defiantly and asked, "So—how did I do?"

"You're actually off to a good start," we told him.

Then we explained that *this question is designed to begin releasing you from the powerful hold that intense, negative thoughts and emotions can have on your ability to think clearly.* Answering thoroughly will help you notice and let go of the full range of your negative feelings.

After that, we gave Scott these coaching cues to help him get the most from his personal answer to Question 1:

Pay attention to all your negative feelings. Your goal here is to notice more than the obvious ones (like anger, hurt, or fear). Look for other subtle and more-difficult-to-acknowledge feelings like jealousy, greed, guilt, shame, help-lessness, or hopelessness. When obvious emotions run high, they can mask other feelings that are operating beneath the surface. If left uncovered, these other feelings can continue to affect how or even whether you will be able to move through the questions. For example, sometimes when we are hurt, we express only anger, but other feelings like disappointment or pain are often there as well.

If you find it difficult to identify the full range of your negative feelings, con-sider one or more of these questions: How do I feel about being angry in this particular situation? When I admit to myself that I am angry, does that thought pull up other feelings like guilt or shame, ongoing frustration, or hopelessness?

Perhaps the problem you are dealing with is a recurring one. In that case, here is a question that can be especially helpful: What negative feelings get triggered in me whenever I'm in this kind of situation? When you know what negative feelings have surged through you before, it's easier to figure out how to keep them from overtaking you the next time you're caught up in a similar situation.

Identify toward whom your feelings are directed. Separate how you feel about your partner from how you feel about yourself. Next to each emotion that you put in your answer, *write down whether that feeling is directed toward your partner or yourself*. When couples are at odds, they tend to focus on and talk about their outwardly directed feelings (anger at a partner, for example). But their inwardly directed emotions (guilt, shame, etc.) are equally important, and being able to discuss these feelings with one another can often lead to effective solutions well worth considering. That is because inwardly directed feelings generally hold the key to our vulnerabilities.

Once you get a handle on what your personal feelings of vulnerability are, you can consider whether or not to share them with your partner. Very often, when you share your vulnerable feelings, you give the other person a more complete understanding of where you are coming from. And when you do that, your partner is likely to respond in a different and more positive way to your request for change.

Replace or remove blaming words. Blaming tends to keep you going round and round in your mind about who's right and who's wrong instead of staying on task and identifying your own negative feelings.

In Scott's initial answer to Question 1, we suggested he change the words *she makes me so angry* to *I am angry*. In other cases, it's best to cross blaming words out altogether like this, *"~~It's all my fault that~~ we fight every morning."*

Fashioning a blame-free description of the problem does two things. It helps you begin to see that you are in charge of your feelings no matter what the other person does or doesn't do. And it's the first step in preparing you to express yourself in a way that makes it easier for your partner to take in and consider your concerns without being distracted by the need to defend past actions.

Eliminate the words *should* **and** *shouldn't*. Although *I should* and *I shouldn't* phrases can pop up automatically, they interfere with your ability to recognize the full range of your genuine feelings. To make this point, we drew Scott's attention toward what happened when his anger at Liz started coming out.

Almost immediately Scott had said, "Maybe I shouldn't be mad at her." And in that moment, Scott short-circuited the full release of his anger.

Get rid of negative labels. Labeling yourself or the other person as *a whiner, selfish, unkind,* or other critical descriptions keeps you focused on the issue of right vs. wrong and limits your ability to explore the broad array of your negative feelings.

In Scott's initial answer, he referred to his efforts as, "whining about something as little as this." We told him he'd get more from his answer by looking back at his words, crossing out any negative labels he found, and returning to the task at hand. Scott agreed to tackle Question 1 again and to incorporate our coaching cues. Here is his more constructive answer:

Question 1:	Scott's More Constructive Answer:	Distracting Thoughts and Worries:
What are my negative feelings?		What do you think I'm feeling?
• Pay attention to all your negative feelings. • Toward whom?	I'm **angry** at Liz because she doesn't do what I'd like her to. I'm **annoyed** at myself for letting this bother me.	And by the way, I **still** think this experiment is absurd!
• Eliminate **should/ shouldn't.** • Replace or remove blaming words. • Get rid of negative labels.	I **resent** the fact that my wife doesn't show me compassion. I'm **embarrassed** that I want her to comfort me. I feel **helpless** to get her to do that.	

Reading over his own words, and realizing that besides anger he felt annoyed, resentful, embarrassed, and helpless Scott said, "You're right; there is a lot more to this than just being pissed off. What's the next question?"

Question 2:	Scott's Initial Answer:	Distracting Thoughts and Worries:
What's the fairest way to describe the problem?	I'm better at comforting than Liz is. She's lousy at it. Maybe I'm just a John Wayne guy who's married to a woman that's not exactly Mother Teresa. Liz probably knows what I want, only it's not in her nature to give it. It's ridiculous to think Liz is going to change after all this time. I'll just have to accept that and force myself to live with the status quo.	

We explained that Question 2 *helps you begin considering your relationship issues from a calmer, less reactive, and more neutral perspective.* Answering this question calls for you to come up with an objective description of your problem as one in which there is a difference in perception, interpretation, personality, styles, or priorities.

Here are the coaching cues we gave Scott to help him restate his problem:

Take out blaming, explaining, or guessing words. While Scott's answer gave us a sense of the problem, his words and energy were so tied-up in: *blaming* ("she's lousy at it"), *explaining* ("I'm a John Wayne guy who married a woman that's not exactly Mother Theresa"), and *guessing* ("Liz probably knows what I want") that he ran the risk of re-igniting his negative feelings instead of beginning to move beyond them.

Remove phrases that imply there's nothing you can do about the problem. Cross out or drop in the margin any statements that suggest you're stuck with things as they are. Then answer this question again using straightforward facts about what is—without any reference to whether you can do anything about the problem. When you do that, you stand a much better chance of initiating positive changes by the time you get to questions three through six.

We pointed out that Scott's last two statements, "It's ridiculous to think Liz is going to change after all this time," and, "I'll just have to accept that and force myself to live with the status quo," reflect his belief that his situation is hopeless and that he is helpless to effect change. This belief, we explained, was keeping him stuck. So we asked him to remove them and suggested that if these or other issues of hopelessness and helplessness crop up again, he drop them into the margin and move on.

Use the word *we* in your answer (as in, "We are different when it comes to…"). This helps you look at and think about a problem as something the two of you *share* instead of a me vs. you issue. Even if it feels artificial to do this, changing the words you use to describe a problem opens you up to the possibility that change can, in fact, take place. And altering your words in this way also helps keep you from falling back into finger pointing or getting stuck in feelings of helplessness.

Ask yourself, What do we usually do when this issue crops up? Notice that this coaching cue simply calls for a straightforward description of the actions you both take. It does not leave any room for you to assume or conclude that the way that you and your spouse react is the only option either of you have.

Now take a look at Scott's more constructive answer:

Question 2:	Scott's More Constructive Answer:	Distracting Thoughts and Worries:
What's the fairest way to describe the problem? • We are different. • No blaming, explaining, or guessing.	As far as my wife and I go, we are different when it comes to our ideas about who's supposed to comfort whom in this marriage. I'd like her to comfort **me** once in a while which she	I still think it's useless to believe that after all these years Liz will change.

Question 2: (cont.)	Scott's More Constructive Answer:	Distracting Thoughts and Worries:
• Remove phrases implying you're stuck. • What do we usually do?	does. This is a pattern that has been going on for more than thirty-four years. And for whatever reason, when I'm down, I end up wishing she would comfort me and, ~~of course~~, she doesn't.	

Surprised, Scott said, "I know nothing is suddenly different here, but describing things without putting the blame on Liz or on me does make me feel calmer."

Question 3:	Scott's Initial Answer:	Distracting Thoughts and Worries:
Why do I want to work things out?	I don't want to **work** things out! I just want the problem to go away!	Stupid question!

We told Scott that *answering this question with as many reasons as you can find to explain why you'd like to settle things—motivates and strengthens your resolve to work through a problem.* We also told him how terrific we thought it was that he realized his thoughts about this question ("Stupid!") could and probably should be dropped into the margin.

Then we gave Scott these coaching cues to help him answer Question 3:

List your *warm and tender feelings* for the other person; *pragmatic thoughts* about the benefits of settling things between you; or *a combination* of these. The more reasons you find, the stronger your motivation and commitment to resolving the problem will be.

Nodding, Scott agreed to answer this question a second time:

Question 3:	Scott's More Constructive Answer:	Distracting Thoughts and Worries:
Why do I want to work things out? • Focus on positive feelings and/or practical reasons.	I want to work this out with Liz because it would really feel good to go home to a wife who comforts me when I'm down. I'd feel less alone with my worries. And I'd be able to concentrate better at work.	

Answering this a second time did not pull up any of Scott's distractions. That's fine. There's no reason to look for things to drop into the margin where none exist.

Question 4:	Scott's Initial Answer:	Distracting Thoughts and Worries:
How would I like things between us to be?	I'd like us to comfort each other. I don't want to feel like our marriage is a one-sided comfort zone.	I'd like Liz to be more like me. I want her to make me feel better when I'm down.

This question *focuses your attention on the realistic and specific things your partner can do to help you resolve the problem.* To answer this question constructively:

Specify the realistic actions you'd like the other person to take. In this case, Scott wanted, "Liz to be more like me," and, "to make me feel better when I'm down." The trouble with Scott's answer is that it sounds nice, but his words are unlikely to give Liz enough information for her to know how to do that. We explained that he'd be more likely to get what he wanted from his wife if he spelled out exactly how he'd like her to comfort him.

To make this point clear, we asked Scott to look at the examples below that compare "nice-sounding, nonspecific descriptions" to other more "realistic and detailed descriptions."

Nice-Sounding, Nonspecific vs. Realistic, Detailed Descriptions	
I'd like us to start having fun together.	I'd like us to go out one night a week and talk about things that make us smile, like a new joke or a movie we liked instead of the bills, our kids, and our jobs.
I just want her to treat me with respect.	I'd like her to smile when she asks me to help with the chores. If I'm in the middle of doing something, I'd like her to ask me when I'll be able to pitch in instead of demanding that I drop what I'm doing and hop to it!
I'd like him to be as thoughtful of me as I am of him.	When he gets home from work, I'd like him to ask me how my day went and tell me about his. And if I tell him I've had a difficult day, I'd like him to help me get dinner ready or offer to do the cooking.

Imagine what the "perfect partner" would do to handle this problem. Thinking about how an ideal person might tackle a problem often makes it easier to identify the practical steps your partner could take to help you settle the problem.

Replace what you *don't* want with a statement about what you *do* want. This helps you lay out the specific actions you would like your partner to take. We addressed Scott's initial answer and pointed out that his words, "I don't want to feel like our marriage is a one-sided comfort zone," tell us what he doesn't want, instead of what he *does* want.

Scott sighed and said, "What I really want is for Liz to put her arms around me when I'm down."

"Great! Put that in your answer," we told him.

"But it doesn't count if I have to ask for that. Liz should do that without me even having to ask her," Scott insisted.

Nevertheless, Scott agreed to try our suggestions. Take a look at his more constructive response:

Question 4:	Scott's More Constructive Answer:	Distracting Thoughts and Worries:
How would I like things between us to be? • Specify your partner's realistic actions. • What would the perfect partner do? • Turn what you **don't** want into what you **do** want.	I'd like both of us to be there for one another when needed. I'd like to get a hug from her when I'm down. I think I'd feel better if that happened. Specifically, when I come home from work, I want Liz to put her arms around me and say, "Aww, you poor guy."	It doesn't count if you have to ask for something like that. She should want to do that without me even asking.

When he completed his answer to Question 4, Scott looked troubled. "Now I know what I want. Big deal! How am I supposed to get Liz to do that?" he asked.

Question 5:	Scott's Initial Answer:	Distracting Thoughts and Worries:
How can I actually get that?	Who knows! Maybe I could walk in the front door tomorrow and announce that I am feeling low and tell her that the least she could do is give me a hug!	Liz's never been a comforting person. I'm an adult; I shouldn't need her to soothe my worries. What if I do this and she acts like she didn't hear me?

Answering this *prepares you to make a specific, blame-free request of your partner and to deal with anything that holds you back.* It's normal to anticipate rejection or to worry that whatever you say will make things worse. But to answer this question effectively, it's important to break free from the worries that hold you back.

To help Scott move forward and stay on task, we gave him these coaching cues:

Decide when, where, and under what circumstances you will set things in motion. Scheduling a time to do this keeps you from putting it off indefinitely. Choosing the place and circumstances in which you will discuss things with your partner lets you move forward in the calmest manner and in the least distracting place. Think about whether there are stressful times during which you should avoid discussions. Perhaps there are times when you know the children will be clamoring for attention. Maybe right before heading off to work is a time best avoided. It might be that late at night you're both just too tired to remain calm.

Specify the actions you will take to handle your problem. By adding in the specific and detailed steps you will take, you begin converting your raw ideas into step-by-step instructions that lead to your goal.

Brainstorm if you're stuck. If the problem you're dealing with is one you've struggled to resolve many times before, you may think, *I've already done everything I can think of.* That's normal. And it can really get in your way here. Even if you're convinced that you've done all that you can to improve things, it's important to look again at the possibilities.

Here are brainstorming fill-in-the-blank statements that have renewed other people's efforts and helped them move forward even after they were certain they'd exhausted every avenue.

Although I'm not yet sure how to get what I want, I could start to try_____
(when?) at _____ **(where?)** and as long as _____
(under what circumstances?).

The advice I would give someone else facing this problem is

_____.

A person who absolutely will not put up with this kind of behavior would

_____

(specific, realistic actions).

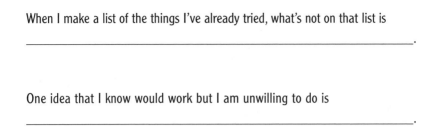

When I make a list of the things I've already tried, what's not on that list is

_____.

One idea that I know would work but I am unwilling to do is

_____.

Keep your goal in mind. Make sure the steps you plan to take will get you what you said you wanted in your answer to Question 4.

Rehearse what you will say and how you will say it in a blame-free manner. This prepares you to communicate in ways that will be easiest for your partner to take in without feeling the need to defend past actions.

- *Review your choice of words in advance.* Keep them direct and blameless.
- *Rehearse out loud or to yourself.* Either way is fine.
- *Notice your tone of voice.*

People tend to respond in a matching tone. Think about it—if someone shouts at you, you're much more likely to answer in anger. If someone speaks to you quietly and directly, your blood doesn't boil nearly as much and your own words are quieter, less demanding.

Describe what you will do to handle the things that worry you most. Look back at what you've dropped into the margin; ask yourself what you will do if the things you're worried about actually happen; include one or more steps that you will take if your concerns materialize.

To show Scott how this works, we asked him to identify his top worry about what might happen when he asks Liz to hug him. Frowning as he thought about this, Scott decided his biggest worry was, "She'll laugh in my face if I ask her to comfort me." Then we asked him, "If Liz laughs in your face, what will you do?"

Scott thought about it for several moments and said, "If she laughs in my face, I'll say, 'Liz, I'm not kidding! I really want you to come over here and hug me.'"

"Great answer!" we told him.

Rehearse again. If the way to handle your worries calls for you to make a direct statement, it's a good idea to rehearse your delivery in advance.

Scott shrugged and insisted we were taking a much too simple approach to what was, for him, a complicated situation. Still, he came up with this more constructive answer:

Question 5:	Scott's More Constructive Answer:	Distracting Thoughts and Worries:
How can I actually get that? • When, where, under what circumstances? • Specify your actions. • Brainstorm if you're stuck. • Keep your goal in mind. • Rehearse blame-free statement. • Handle worries. • Rehearse again.	I guess I can go home tomorrow and say, "I've had an awful day at work. I feel like I'm the worst human-resources executive in the world. So, I'd like you to come over here, put your arms around me, and say, 'Aww, you poor guy.'" If Liz laughs in my face I'll say, "Liz, I'm not kidding! I really want you to give me a hug."	It doesn't count if I have to ask for this. She should want to do this without me asking. She'll think I'm weak and she'll be disgusted.

Hearing from the other group members that his words and his tone of voice were clear and blameless, Scott smiled and we moved on to the last question.

Question 6:	Scott's Initial Answer:	Distracting Thoughts and Worries:
And if that doesn't work, what else can I do?	"Hell, if all else fails, I'll record myself saying, 'Aww, you poor guy'. Then I can listen to my own voice whenever I want some sympathy!"	

We explained that answering Question 6 *gives people a solid back-up plan to use if their first plan doesn't work.* Back-up plans come in many forms ranging from alternative ways to work things out with your partner to strategies to handle things on your own. Even if you never use your back-up plan, just knowing that you have one can be enough to keep you calm and focused should things get tense and/or your partner is unwilling to give you what you want.

Scott didn't look at all convinced. In fact, he seemed so unwilling to come up with a back-up plan that we made the following suggestions:

Pick a realistic time, place, and circumstances to put your back-up plan into motion. If your first plan meets with failure, will you implement your back-up plan immediately or several days later? Will you need time to calm down? If so, how much time? Be specific.

Specify the actions you will take to address your problem.

Keep your goal in mind. Look at your initial answer and ask, "Will this plan *really* get you what you said you wanted in your answer to Question 4? If not, come up with another one!

Reviewing his answer to this question, "I'd like to get a hug from her when I'm down." Scott agreed that taping his voice was a far cry from getting a hug from his wife.

Include the steps you will take to handle your remaining worries. Look at what you dropped into the margin (as you did when you answered Question 5). In this case, Scott found that he continued to worry that Liz will "sense weakness in me and be disgusted," or that "I'll sound like a child asking his mommy to take care of him."

Once again, ask yourself what you'll do if the things you're worried about actually happen. Specify one or more steps you will take if your concerns materialize.

Rehearse what you'll say and how you'll say it in a blame-free manner. Rehearsing out loud or in your head, pay attention to your words and tone of voice.

Moments later, Scott came up with this more constructive answer:

Question 6:	Scott's More Constructive Answer:	Distracting Thoughts and Worries:
And if that doesn't work, what else can I do? • When, where, under what circumstances? • Specify your actions. • Keep your goal in mind. • Rehearse blame-free statement. • Handle worries. • Rehearse again.	I'll wait a week to cool down. Then, when **she** needs comforting, I'll do it just like I'd want her to comfort me. Later I'll say, "Liz when you're upset, I try my best to comfort you. And there are times when I'd like you to hug me and say the same kinds of things I say to you when you feel down." Then I'll look her in the eye. If she seems receptive, I'll keep going and say, "Would you do that for me?"	After I've comforted her, Liz won't laugh or act disgusted by what I have to say. And I won't sound like a child asking his mother to take care of him.

When Scott finished speaking, the others in the room clapped and we thanked him for helping us present the basic questions.

"That's it? That's all there is to this whole approach?" Scott asked incredulously.

"Yes, that's it. You've gone through the basic questions and you answered each one thoroughly. We're impressed with what you did. Thanks!" we told him.

Scott took a deep breath and announced, "If you say so. But I'm not convinced your approach will work, and I'm not making any promises about how this will turn out."

Outcome

The next week, Scott phoned and said, "On the way home from your workshop, I thought about how I'd been wanting and not asking my wife for comfort for years. That never worked and it probably never would. I knew it was time to do things differently. So I walked into my house, stood up tall, and told Liz I'd had a rotten day. Then I asked her to wrap her arms around me and say 'Aww, you poor guy.'"

"What happened when you did that?" we asked.

"Liz looked stunned. She didn't move. Finally, I had to say, 'Really, I mean it, Liz. Come over here.' She walked over to me slowly, gave me a quick hug, rushed through the words, 'Aww, you poor guy,' and backed away as fast as she could.

"'No, not like that,' I told her. 'I want you to do it again, only this time I want you to pretend that you're the grandest earth mother in the universe.' So she did and she really hammed it up. I knew Liz was play-acting, but I was really starting to feel better. And that's when it dawned on me; even if you come right out and ask someone to give you what you want, getting it from them *does* count, if you let it."

Observations

Even if you're dealing with a long-standing issue (like Scott's thirty-four years of low-level resentment because Liz didn't comfort him) and even if you're convinced nothing you can do will change things, tracking your personal answers to the six questions and following the coaching cues laid out in this chapter can shift your focus from what *won't* work to what *might work*. And from there, you're on your way to getting unstuck without coming unglued!

WHEN IT IS TIME TO TALK: FINDING YOUR VOICE

While there is no one-size-fits-all answer to the problems they face, the people whose stories follow found that writing their answers to the six questions helped them get past their disputes more calmly and effectively than they'd thought possible. In fact, most told us that their negative feelings and concerns lessened or disappeared altogether. And quite a few went on to say that something about answering the questions left them feeling so relaxed that they were able to pick up and run with some wonderful, unanticipated, and creative solutions. We believe that the "something" they referred to is the relaxed state of mind people enter after they have addressed their worries.

We also noticed that by answering the basic questions, those men and women with whom we worked found it easier than they'd imagined to initiate a discussion about the problem with their partner (even when the issue was delicate, potentially explosive, or highly emotional).

As one woman put it, "Now I know *what* I'd like my husband to do and exactly *how* I'd like him to do it. I've practiced a blame-free way to ask him for that and I've got a great way to bring the whole thing up. So I'm not as worried about how he and I are going to work through this as I was before!"

The truth is, no matter how many times we assure you that tracking your answers to the basic questions will prepare you to talk calmly with your partner (without falling into the familiar cycle of shouting back, shutting down, or racing for the hills), until you've experienced this for yourself, you're likely to remain unconvinced.

For that reason, below you will find a few things that have helped other equally unconvinced people to find their voice, hang in there as the discussion unfolds, and then take positive steps to settle their relationship problem(s):

Preparation
Jot down key points. Write them on a note card and check off each one as you cover it.

Setting and Timing
Minimize distractions. Begin the conversation where you're unlikely to be disturbed. Choose a time when neither of you is preoccupied with other pressing life events.

Increase the Likelihood That Your Words Will Get Through
Describe your desired outcome. Let your partner know what you hope the end result of your discussion will be. Express your genuine, positive reasons for wanting to work things out. This reassures others that you're neither looking to escalate your disagreement nor end your relationship.

Be prepared to listen. Your willingness to hear from your partner signals that you welcome and value his or her reactions, concerns, and insights.

Enroll your partner. Invite him or her to make suggestions about how you might solve things together.

And If You Still Feel Stuck or Tempted to Give Up

Think out loud. In front of your partner, say what's on your mind as if you are speaking aloud to yourself. For example, you might say, "I want this to work out because I care about you and I'm worried that if I toss in the towel, we'll end up even farther apart."

Put your nonblaming request in a letter. Then give or mail it to your partner. This will give you time to carefully choose your blame-free words, state your positive reasons for wanting to work things out, and describe the outcome you hope for.

Follow Through

Take action. Put your plan into motion just as you rehearsed it. In order to alter or improve a relationship, at some point you have to put one foot in front of the other and move off in a new direction. We encourage you to do that sooner rather than later.

WHAT YOU WILL FIND IN THE REST OF THIS BOOK:

The next chapter shows you how to use the six questions to address the little things that can crop up and erode even the best of relationships. And the chapter after that, "What If Your Partner Won't Budge?" demonstrates how to use the basic questions to keep moving toward a positive end-result even if your partner won't cooperate.

After that, each chapter examines a different type of couples' conflict. These include disputes about finances, parenting styles, religious beliefs, in-laws, infidelity, and more. Nearly every chapter contains a story that describes, in detail, how a person has successfully managed to work through a problem with a non-cooperative partner.

To help you keep the basic questions and coaching cues in mind, at the start of each chapter we'll show you how one person applied his or her written answers in especially effective ways.

In the chapters that address the kinds of deeply troubling issues that cannot be resolved and may, in fact, put a marriage at risk, you'll find examples of how people have applied the coaching cues to move beyond their intense emotional upheaval and on toward realistic, productive options. Getting past deeply hurtful conflicts very often requires two things: the willingness to connect with and remain connected to your sense of goodwill and the ability to keep your eyes on the prize. In the chapters to come, you will hear from people who used the basic questions to do that in creative, effective, and sometimes amazing ways.

As you read all these stories, we hope you will begin to think about the problems that you and your partner face with a sense of hopefulness and a greater appreciation for your own ability to effect positive change. And we also hope you'll notice that writing your personal answers to the six questions—using the format laid out for you in this chapter—makes doing this easier. (In the appendix you will find a sample worksheet to use as a guide when you are ready to start doing this yourself.)

3

It's the Little Things!

When everyday irritations build up and boil over

"So I ask him to take out the trash, and he acts like he's doing me a favor."

"We get in the car, and she turns into the back-seat driver from hell."

"Just once I want him to do something for me without asking for a favor in return."

"She's always asking me, 'Do I look fat in this dress?' What am I supposed to say?"

Sound familiar? Most of us have heard remarks like these. We may even have uttered them ourselves. After all, no matter how kind, understanding, or polite we may be, there are going to be times when the "little things" our partner does irritate, upset, offend, disappoint, or hurt us. It comes with the territory.

So how do couples hold on to their warm and tender feelings for each other when everyday little things crop up? You are about to hear how four people whose nerves were frayed and whose teeth were clenched over the little things—did just that.

What I Learned from Barbra Streisand

Caroline is the director of a large university library. She's married to a well-known trial attorney and she laughingly describes her married life as an exercise in finding new ways to get off the witness stand. Below, Caroline details a problem she had with her husband, Jim, and explains how the basic questions helped her:

"Jim's office is around the corner from the pharmacy where we have a charge account. One night, I asked if he'd stop by the pharmacy on his way home the next day to pick up a prescription for me. Jim said he couldn't do that because he wasn't going to be working at his office that day.

"'No problem,' I said, and opened my appointment book to write myself a reminder to take care of it myself.

"Then Jim looked up at me (I swear I could almost see the wheels turning in his lawyer head) and said, 'I'll make you a deal; I'll pick up your medicine if you'll stop by the cleaners and pick up my shirts.'

"I nodded, only for some reason I felt irritated. Throughout most of the next day, I felt annoyed and I didn't know why. I kept looking at my watch—worried I might forget to pick up his damn shirts. After work, I headed for the cleaners but there was so much traffic that it looked like I might not get there on time. Trapped in a snarl of cars I felt myself beginning to boil.

"The drugstore stays open late. The cleaners closed in fifteen minutes! Why couldn't Jim have picked up my medicine without turning it into one of those 'I'll do this for you if you do something else for me' things? If I don't get to the cleaners before they close, he'll be mad and I'll feel like a screw up. *Why* couldn't he just do something for *me* when I asked him without turning it into a negotiation?

"I was loaded with resentment toward Jim for turning my request into a tit-for-tat bargain! I'd rather have gotten my own medicine than deal with his stupid dry cleaning. I was mad at myself, annoyed with Jim, and aggravated by all the rush-hour noise, smells, and rudeness when it hit me…there I was, sitting in my car answering Question 1: What are my negative feelings? At the time, that was the only one of your questions I could remember.

"The traffic finally unclogged and I got to the cleaners with five minutes to spare. When I got home, we swapped medicine for shirts. Both of us said, 'Thank you,' but I didn't mean it. Not that Jim noticed.

"Later on, we were watching TV but the whole hassle of the day was still bothering me, so I picked up your book again and sat down at my desk to reread the questions. I thought you'd be interested in seeing my answers, so here you go:"

Questions:	Answers:	Distracting Thoughts and Worries:
1. What are my negative feelings?	**Mad** at myself, **annoyed** with Jim and **confused**.	
2. What's the fairest way to describe the problem?	We're different when it comes to doing a favor. When Jim asks me to do something, I say 'yes' or 'no'. When I ask him, he trades my request for one of his own.	I hate when he turns my requests into a way to get something for himself.
3. Why do I want to work things out?	I love Jim. I just don't like the way he does a few things.	
4. How would I like things between us to be?	Sometimes I'd like a favor… not a negotiation—not even a reasonable negotiation. Next time I make a request, I'd like Jim to give me a simple 'yes' or 'no.'	
5. How can I actually get that?	I don't know how to bring it up without having it turn into an argument. I wish I was like Barbra Streisand in the movie **The Way We Were**, where she and Robert Redford break up and later she phones him and says, 'Hubble, I have a problem. I need to talk to you because you're my best friend. Only this problem of mine is about you. So, would you just be my best friend now and pretend we're talking about a	

Questions:	Answers:	Distracting Thoughts and Worries:
	problem I'm having with somebody else?' I loved that way of talking about a problem.	
	"Suppose I dialed Jim's cell phone and said, 'Look, right now I may not need a husband but I sure do need a friend?' Then I could tell him about this problem I'm having with my best friend, a great guy named Jim who always asks for a favor in return when I make a request.	I could do this!
6. And if that doesn't work what else can I do?	I could wait 'til this comes up again because now I think it comes up more often than I realized. And then I could tell Jim that all I want him to do is give me a 'yes' or a 'no' and not to attach any strings to my request.	Trouble is, I'd have to remember to say, 'Give me a "yes" or a "no."' I'm not great at remembering things like that.

Outcome

"After I answered the questions, I walked back into the den with my cell phone and called Jim on his. It was funny. We were both sitting on the couch in the den—right next to each other talking into our phones. But I kept my back to him so I could concentrate on the words without seeing his reaction.

"I started telling him how crazed I'd been all day long just because 'my very dearest friend in the whole world,' a man named Jim, was complicating my life in ways he probably didn't even know!

"I told him how annoyed at myself I'd been for agreeing to pick up his shirts. And that I now realized I'd wanted him to pick up my medicine without asking me to do something for him in return. 'I didn't even know that's what I wanted until I got stuck in an awful traffic jam,' I explained.

"'I don't always feel that way,' I said, 'just sometimes. So when I really want a gift, not a tit-for-tat, what do you think I should do?'

"Jim's reaction really threw me. He shook his head and said, 'You're amazing. All that over a trip to the dry cleaners?'

"I thought maybe he was suggesting that I was making a big deal out of nothing. I felt embarrassed and defensive and almost said, 'How dare you sit there and suggest I'm overreacting!'

"But I kept thinking about what I really wanted and that I didn't want to get sidetracked, so instead I said, 'Look, it's a little thing to you but it's a big one to me. What am I supposed to do if I want you to do something for me without you adding any conditions onto what I want?'

"'Well, just say, "I am asking for a gift not a negotiation."'

"'Okay, I'll do that,' I said.

"'And if I want something with no strings attached from you, I get to do the same thing, is that the deal?' he asked.

"'That's the deal,' I said with a smile, realizing that Jim was negotiating again and suddenly I didn't mind it a bit."

Observations

We especially liked two things about Caroline's approach to the six questions. When she had trouble answering Question 5 (*How can I actually get that?*), what Caroline didn't write is as important as what she did write. Many of us might have used the words, *I can't do this*, but Caroline wrote, *I don't know how*.

The difference between *I can't* and *I don't know how* is enormous. Saying "I can't" leaves us with nowhere to go. Saying, "I don't know how," leaves us open to look for ways to proceed. And when Caroline still had trouble with Question 5, she instinctively asked herself what someone else facing the same problem might do. This is, in fact, a version of the *What would the perfect partner do?* coaching cue that we presented in more detail in chapter 2.

Thinking about how someone else might respond to a problem frees people from the belief that nothing they can do will work. And it releases them from their worries about how the other person will respond. After that, it becomes a good deal easier for people to identify the specific steps they can take to get what they want or need from their partners.

She's Driving Me Crazy

As the following story demonstrates, creating constructive answers to the basic questions does not require you to write at length, nor does it call for you to be particularly insightful.

Dennis, a coffee-shop acquaintance who married his high-school sweetheart, Marsha, often shows us photos from the high-adventure vacations he and his wife enjoy. Generally, Dennis points to some picture of Marsha and with sparkling eyes says, "Look at my wife. Isn't she amazing? Aren't women one of God's best ideas?"

That's why we were particularly startled when Dennis sidled over to our table one morning and with a halfway apologetic nod toward JacLynn, uttered this one-word complaint: "Women!"

Before we could say a thing, Dennis rushed on:

"You know that old saying about a good fight clears the air? Bull! Marsha and I have the same fight every week and believe me—it never does any good! We get into it every time we go out for the evening. Usually we're headed to the movies. She has night blindness, so I drive," he explained.

"We get in the car, all smiles, really looking forward to our night out. But before we've gone a mile, she's clutching the handle on her side of the car yelling, 'Watch out!' and stomping the floor with her right foot as if she could stop the car from the passenger's side!

"I get so rattled; I grip the steering wheel and tell her to cut it out! I say, 'I'm going below the speed limit for crying out loud!' But then she starts saying things like, 'You're supposed to come to a complete stop, not just slow down at the intersection,' or, 'Watch it—you're too close to the car in front,' or, 'You're driving like a maniac!' And then I get so pissed that I tell her to 'shut up or she's going to get us both killed.'

"By the time we get to the theater, we're not even talking to each other. Some fun, huh? The night's ruined and mind you, I still have to drive us both back home!

"Got anything in your book to get wives to back off when you're at the wheel?"

"Not yet," we chuckled. "Interested in trying our approach to see if it helps?"

"Yeah, I guess," Dennis said.

Occasionally, Dennis referred to the coaching cues in chapter 2 as he answered the basic questions. Here are his answers:

Question 1: What are my negative feelings?

I've got to answer this without blaming right? Okay, let's see, I get annoyed every time she does this because it ruins the whole night. I'm frustrated and I keep feeling like, "Here we go again." And I'm mad at myself for shouting back because that just makes things worse.

Question 2: What's the fairest way to describe the problem?

I'm going to try answering this question by saying, "We are different when it comes to..." Um, obviously we don't agree about whether or not my driving is any good. And we're clearly different in our ideas about how a passenger is supposed to behave.

Question 3: Why do I want to work things out?

Because except for this fight, Marsha and I have fun together. Always have.

Question 4: How would I like things between us to be?

I'd like us to stop fighting when we're on our way somewhere in the car! I know, I know—that's not what you call a "realistic and detailed description," is it? Let me think for a sec. All right, how about this? The next time we get in the car together and I'm the one who's driving, I'd like her to relax. If she can't, then I'd like her to quietly and gently say something like, "I'm getting nervous. Would you humor me and slow down a bit?"

Question 5: How can I actually get that?

Before we leave the house next time, I could say, "Let's both try to get to the movie theater in a good mood tonight. How about if you start getting freaked out about my driving—instead of hollering at each other like we usually do— would you say something like, "Honey, humor me here and slow down 'til we get there?"

Question 6: And if that doesn't work, what else can I do?

Lord, I dunno. Um—okay, here's something…I could just cut to the heart of things and—before we leave the house—tell her that if she gets scared while I'm driving to just sing that song—you know, the one that goes, "Slow down, you move too fast?"

That way, even if she sings off key at the top of her lungs, I won't get as mad as I do when she's yelling at me!

Outcome

The next time that we saw Dennis, he gave us the thumbs up and said, "It worked!"

Observations

We think Dennis's success stems from his ability to make a detailed and specific request of his wife ("Would you say something like, 'Honey, humor me and slow down 'til we get there?'") In making his request, Dennis gave Marsha a concrete and practical way to get what she wanted. And in the process, he got what he wanted too—a way to enjoy his evenings out with his wife!

A Heavy Question

Glenn, Paul's patient, had been married for just over five years when he told Paul how worried he was about his wife, Melody. Apparently, Melody had gained a great deal of weight over the past two years and seemed terribly distressed about her appearance. Glenn said he felt hopeless about being able to help her—or cheer her up or even reassure her that he loved her. When Paul told him about the basic questions, Glenn decided to put his answers in a personal letter to his wife. Although Glenn didn't actually write the basic questions in the body of his letter, we've placed them in parentheses throughout his letter to show you how he answered each one.

Glenn did something in his letter that we want you to notice. He changed the wording of one of the questions to fit his particular situation. Rather than ask and answer Question 5 as it is (*How can I actually get that?*), Glenn reworded this question and instead asked, "How can I actually *give* that?"

We liked the way Glenn made that question his own. While the changes in wording are subtle—it seems to us that they add depth and meaning to his letter. Here is what Glenn wrote:

Dear Melody,

I got home before you did today. I was trying to read the newspaper but I couldn't. I kept thinking about what you asked me last night—"Why don't I just leave you?" Your question made me so angry (What are my negative feelings?) *that I didn't trust myself to answer you right then. Now I'm calmer.*

(What's the fairest way to describe the problem?) *For months, you've been asking me how you look in one outfit after another. I don't know how to answer without hurting your feelings. When I tell you that you look great, it doesn't help because we both know that isn't true. When I say I think another outfit would be better, you slam out of the room. But if I say you look good to me— you give me that look of yours which means you don't believe me. I can't think of anything else to say so I am writing this because talking about it hasn't gone too well for us.*

You've started asking me if your weight is a turnoff to me. (Why do I want to work things out?) *I want to answer this now so we can go back to being happy together. I'm writing this out so you can read it over again whenever you doubt my feelings for you. Melody, I love you just as much today as I did on our wedding day. I'm not going to leave you and I am not going to give up on you or our marriage because I love you no matter what you weigh. That isn't going to change. I am not, I repeat NOT, going anywhere.*

Do I wish you were thinner? Yes I do. That is true, but not for the reasons you probably think. I wish you were thinner because I miss the "you" that used to be happy with yourself. Melody, I miss the sound of your laughter. I miss you feeling so good about yourself that I couldn't wait to get home to you. Your happiness is a real turn-on to me. That's the truth.

I know how it feels to look in the mirror and not like what you see because as you know, I used to be fat.

For most of my life, my self-confidence was nonexistent. I covered that up by being funny and working hard to be someone others could count on to help or fix things in a crisis. I got good at taking charge, just not good at taking charge of my own life.

Years ago, I even told a therapist that I was afraid no one would ever marry me. I never told you that. But for a long time I really didn't think anyone—certainly not you—would ever want to be married to someone like me. It wasn't just because of my weight that I thought that. It was also because, let's face it, I am sort of an oddball.

I was grateful when you said you'd marry me. Being your husband has changed a lot of things for me. When we got married, I felt so happy and confident that even at work, people noticed a change. I also felt so good about myself (thanks to you) that I started working out again and finally got my weight under control. I know that my being thinner than you only aggravates things between us. I don't know what to do about that.

(How would I like things between us to be?) *I'd like to give you the confidence that being married to you has given to me. I want to do that, but I can't. Nobody can give that to another person no matter how much they want to.* (How can I actually *give* that?) *All I can give you is my absolute belief in your ability to get that for yourself. In the meantime, I hope my faith in you makes things easier.* (And if that doesn't work, what else can I do?) *I'm staying right here with you, Melody.*

I love you. And I always will.

Glenn

Outcome

Some time after Glenn gave Melody his letter, he told Paul, "I left my letter on Melody's desk and went out to run some errands. When I got back, Melody was already home. She'd read my letter and was pretty choked up but in a good way.

And that letter got us talking about her eating problems. Melody's thinking about seeing a specialist.

I said whatever she wants to do I'd back her 100 percent. Nothing much has changed since then except Melody is more relaxed around me and more affectionate too—which, come to think of it, is a pretty big change."

Observations

We have found that there can be enormous value in creating written messages for the people we love, especially when we are dealing with sensitive or hard-to-talk-about topics. Putting our thoughts down on paper gives us time to choose our words carefully, lets the receiver absorb them in private, and reduces the likelihood that our intentions will be misinterpreted.

Who Does What at Home?

This account shows that even when your written responses appear to be "off the mark," taking the time to ask and answer all six questions can help you communicate your concerns to your partner more effectively and clearly than you previously have.

Karen is a grade-school science teacher. She and her husband, Craig, have been married for eleven years. They married late in life and have no children. According to Karen, for most of her married life, she's held a grudge against her husband.

"Asking Craig to do anything around the house is a waste of breath," she harrumphs regularly. Then she goes on to say, "He's always saying, 'Yeah, yeah, I'll do it later.' But 'later' takes forever with him! So either I have to keep reminding him over and over or I get so impatient that I do it myself. Then I grumble loudly about it to make sure he knows *I'm* doing what he said *he'd* do. If I can stand to wait him out long enough, he finally does one thing, and then he acts like he's done me a big favor!

"I've had years and years of therapy. I already *know* I'm what they call an 'enabler,' which means what I do makes it possible for Craig to keep doing what he's doing—outwait me until I end up doing all the work around our house. But at least that lets me make sure Craig sees me doing all the things he should be doing!

"*Why* do I need Craig to see that? I guess I want him to appreciate all that I do at home to sort of give me equal footing in his eyes. Craig makes a lot more money than I do. Even though I love teaching, let's be honest here—I'll never come close to contributing as much money to our lives as he can! I'm afraid Craig might think that bringing home less money makes me less than his equal partner."

Take a look at where Karen's answers led her:

Question 1: What are my negative feelings?
Irritation. Exasperation. Resentment. I feel all of that toward Craig.

Question 2: What's the fairest way to describe the problem?
We are different when it comes to who does what at home. Craig avoids. I complain. Then I give up and do it myself. But don't think I don't let him know all the things I'm doing around the house! Okay, so I'm enabling Craig. So what?

Question 3: Why do I want to work things out?
I love Craig. I like being married to him. But every once in a while, when I hear what's coming out of my mouth, I'm afraid that I'm turning into my mother. She used to light into my father and me all the time about us not doing our chores. It was a drag. I don't want to be like her—not in that way. But while I *know* that, all the insight in the world doesn't tell you *how* to change things, now does it?

But this really isn't a big deal. I mean, every wife complains about her husband— that's the way it is. At least that gives me something to talk about with the other teachers. And, like I said, at home my complaining lets me make sure Craig knows what I do to keep things running smoothly is important.

Question 4: How would I like things between us to be?
I'd like us both to do things around the house without me having to bug him. But even if Craig did all the things I keep harping about, that's only part of what I'd like. The other part is that I'd like Craig to assure me that even if I never make as much money as he does, I am just as important as he is in this marriage.

Question 5: How can I actually get that?

I could be more patient. Let Craig do his chores when he's ready. Maybe just leave his dirty clothes where they are or let the trash bags pile up until he gets around to them. But that won't get Craig to appreciate the things I do at home.

Question 6: And if that doesn't work, what else can I do?

Go back into therapy, I suppose. But even if I *do* that, I'd still like to stop bugging Craig, and I'd still want him to tell me I'm just as worthwhile as he is—even if he always out-earns me. I wish I'd come up with an idea about something to do that would make things nicer for both of us. I know how to do that for the students in my classroom. I've got this chart with all their names on it at the back of the room, and when they complete their work I put gold stars next to their names. Each time anyone gets ten stars, he or she gets a night with no homework. The kids like that. So do I. But making a chart for a husband and wife? Would Craig go for something like that? No, he'd think it was just another way for me to pick on him.

Outcome

As far as we could tell, Karen's answers hadn't produced the kinds of concrete, practical action plans that we'd come to expect. And for a while, we wondered if Karen might be an example of that old saying, "There's an exception to every rule." However, weeks later we learned that the basic questions had so deeply affected Karen that she and her husband had taken steps to improve things immediately. It just took her longer to tell us that!

Here is what Karen said happened after she'd answered the questions:

"Craig and I were having one of those nights with me asking for help and him saying 'later, later,' when I just lost it and started sobbing. I never do that. Poor Craig—he looked so worried. He kept saying, 'Honey, honey what is it? What's wrong?' But I was crying so hard that it took me a while to answer him.

"Finally, I said I was tired of always hounding him to do things around the house. I said it made me feel like a shrew. And then I admitted that all I really wanted was for him to help out a little bit more and to appreciate what I did at home. Since he was the big bread winner and I made so little money,

I felt like I needed to prove to both of us that I was an equal partner in this marriage.

"Craig kept saying, 'Shh, shh—don't cry.'

"'What're we going to do?' I wailed. 'I only know how to get kids to want to do things—not husbands!'

"'So, I'm a kid—just a big one. What works with the small ones?' he asked.

"I told him about the chart I use at school and we ended up making a chart that has both our names and a list of the household chores on it. And now, every time either of us does one of the chores, we put a star by our name. When we get to ten, we get a reward.

"My reward is Craig tells me five things he appreciates about me. His reward is that I give him a five-minute foot massage. So far, I have heard forty reasons Craig appreciates me. Craig has gotten three foot massages. We're both happier, and the house stays clean. Not bad for a school teacher, now is it?"

Observations

According to Karen, this was the first time she was able to tell Craig the truth about her frustrations without blaming or berating him. Doing that helped Craig take in her words without feeling the need to protect himself from an attack and helped him empathize with his wife. Then, together they turned Karen's idea of using a chart into a fully developed plan with built-in rewards for both of them.

THOUGHTS TO TAKE WITH YOU

We hope the stories you have just read encourage you to start using the basic questions to settle your differences before the little things turn into big ones! To help, it's a good idea to:

- Swap the words *I can't* for the words *I don't know how.*
- Answer each question fully (the length of your answers is unimportant).
- Identify your below-the-surface feelings (Question 1).
- Consider letter writing when the topic is hard to talk about in person.
- Be diligent about communicating in a blame-free manner.

4

What If Your Partner Won't Budge?

Moving ahead together anyway

Suppose the two of you are at odds over something you feel strongly about. Now suppose that no matter what you do or say, you can't get your partner to go along with what you want. Where do you go from there? Can the basic questions help you settle things without your partner's cooperation? Yes, more often than you think!

You are about to hear from three women whose answers to the questions helped them calm their anger and frustration at their partners' unwillingness to budge, get clear about exactly what it was they wanted, and take steps to get that. These women found themselves caught up in the kinds of conflict situations that most of us would think can only be resolved if both people work together. And yet, with little or no cooperation from their partners, they found ways to settle their differences and move on together.

The first woman's story centers on her partner's reluctance to discuss ways to improve their lovemaking. The second woman's account describes her husband's failure to live up to his promise to train their new pet. And the third story shows how a woman coped with her husband's flat-out refusal to stop smoking.

Obviously these are by no means the only kinds of couple's conflicts in which one partner's unwillingness to budge can stop you in your tracks. In nearly every chapter of this book, you'll find accounts from men and women who were embroiled in a wide range of seemingly "unresolvable" disputes about everything from money to annoying personal habits, interfering ex-spouses, meddling in-laws, religious differences, infidelity, and more.

What we want you to get from reading these personal accounts is this: Even if your partner is reluctant, resistant, or flat-out refuses to cooperate—all is not lost. By tracking your personal answers to the six basic questions, you—all by yourself—really can alter the tone and improve the outcome of a dispute.

Adored but Bored

Below, you will hear from a young married woman who meets a great deal of resistance from her husband when she tries to get him to change the way they make love. This is what Penny, a twenty-six-year-old woman whom we met when we spoke at a daylong seminar about intimacy, told us:

"I tried to get my husband, Warren, to come with me today, but he said, 'No way. I'm not going to discuss our private business in front of strangers!'"

Penny sighed, "The trouble is, Warren won't discuss it in private with me either. He says sex was not talked about in his house when he was growing up and he prefers that it not be discussed in his home now. But I think we need to talk about it because our sex life is so predictable that it's boring.

"Warren is good guy. He loves me, and I love him, too. He's a few years older than me, but he's a whole lot more uptight. I've got plenty of ideas about how to spice things up. But he won't let me get past the first syllable of a description before he's out of earshot.

"The last time I tried to plant a few ideas in his head was a month ago. I just sauntered up to him one morning and in a sexy voice asked him how he'd like it if I painted his body with chocolate sauce and licked it off. Poor Warren was so discombobulated he couldn't speak. He just shook his head 'no' and raced out of the house to go to work.

"I have tried all kinds of ways to get him to talk about this. One time, I even wrote to an advice columnist and asked her what to do. I signed my letter 'adored but bored.' When the answer to my question showed up in the newspaper a few weeks later, I showed it to Warren without letting on that I'd written the question. He read it and handed the newspaper back to me without a word! And that was the end of that.

"I wish I knew how to talk to him about trying new things without freaking him out. So I guess that's why I'm here today."

Penny's written responses to the basic questions and the coaching cues that she found most helpful are presented below:

Question 1:	Penny's Answer:	Distracting Thoughts and Worries:
What are my negative feelings? • Toward whom? • Eliminate **should/ shouldn't**.	I feel **lonely** and **irritated** at Warren when he starts in on his same old way of letting me know he wants to make love. Then my **guilt** kicks in. ~~I think about all the good things about Warren and I think I shouldn't complain about something as small as this.~~	Something's missing. Like in that movie **Pleasantville**, I feel as if I'm living in black and white and wishing for color.

Question 2:	Penny's Answer:	Distracting Thoughts and Worries:
What's the fairest way to describe the problem? • What do we usually do?	Our sex life is boring. Usually when we discuss this Warren says, "I don't want to talk about it." So I've stopped bringing it up, but the problem hasn't gone away. I still want to find a way to spice up our lovemaking.	What's Warren's problem? You'd think I wanted to talk to him about whips and chains instead of chocolate nipples and edible underwear.

Question 3:	Penny's Answer:	Distracting Thoughts and Worries:
Why do I want to work things out? • Focus on positive feelings and/or practical reasons.	We've got so many things going for us that if we could just add a little spark to our lovemaking and be more playful with each other ~~instead of being so serious all the time~~ things would be perfect. Then I could put all the things I've read about and the new sex toys I know are out there to use. Besides, anything that adds passion to our marriage can't help but be good for both of us.	What if he won't ever try something new?

Question 4:	Penny's Answer:	Distracting Thoughts and Worries:
How would I like things between us to be? • Specify your partner's realistic actions. • What would the perfect partner do?	I'd like ~~our lovemaking to be less predictable and~~ to make love on a different day of the week, at a different time of night, even in a different room than usual. The perfect partner would bring new ideas to lovemaking. He'd suggest long bubble baths, slow dancing in the kitchen while our food is cooking, etc. He'd be willing to try new things.	Answering this makes me sad. Warren doesn't act like my idea of a "perfect partner." Can he change? I'm afraid he won't.

Question 5:	Penny's Answer:	Distracting Thoughts and Worries:
How can I actually get that? • When, where, and under what circumstances? • Specify your actions. • Handle worries.	I can do what I did once before when I rubbed his shoulders and one thing led to another. Tonight, I can give him a glass of wine, hand him my new bottle of flavored massage oil, and ask him to massage my back. That way, if he doesn't respond, I can act as if I only wanted him to rub my back. Then I won't feel like a fool. And if this does work, I can try other things and maybe keep things interesting for a long time.	I know not to greet him wearing only cellophane. If I try this without talking to him first, will he get bent out of shape? Is it going to turn him off? What if he just rubs my back but doesn't go beyond that?

Question 6:	Penny's Answer:	Distracting Thoughts and Worries:
And if that doesn't work what else can I do? • Specify your actions. • Keep your goal in mind.	I can always go into my own head and just **let my fantasies turn me on**. I know I said I wanted Warren to make love to me on a different day of the week, at a different time of night, and in a different room than we usually do. And no—this won't get me that. But **it will give me a way to imagine it**—and that might just be as good as it gets.	The trouble with this idea is that when I turn to my fantasies about things, I end up alone with my thoughts instead of being right there with Warren.

Outcome

Some months later, we heard this from Penny:

"I didn't expect the things I wrote at the seminar to be much help to me when I got home. So I was really surprised when my idea about asking him to rub my lower back worked. Then I thought—well, if that worked, maybe I should try some of the other things I wrote down. (I'm glad I kept my basic question worksheets.)

"So the next thing I tried was the dancing in the kitchen idea. I waited until a night when Warren came home in a fairly good mood. Then I put the radio in the kitchen on and turned it to my favorite station. Warren was just hanging up his coat when a slow song we both like came on. I asked him if he'd dance with me. He did and then some!

"I was lucky that song came on when it did, but if I hadn't thought about things in advance I wouldn't even have turned the radio on. Anyway, I guess you can tell that things are less boring for me now."

Observations

Penny's answers to the six questions seem to support that old saying: "actions speak louder than words." When all her efforts to get Warren to discuss making the kinds of changes she wanted weren't leading anywhere, Penny shifted her focus and concentrated instead on creating low-key romantic situations that could lead directly to the actions she desired. Doing that made it easier for Warren to try new things.

What we especially liked about Penny's solution is that it took into account both Warren's reluctance to discuss their intimate lives *and* her own worries about being rebuffed (*"That way, if he doesn't respond, I can act as if I only wanted him to rub my back. Then, I won't feel like a fool."*).

Doggone It!

Here is another example of how a person found a way to solve things on her own when her partner would not cooperate.

Carole and Keith have been married for three years. They have a ten-month-old son named Harry. Carole put her career on hold to become a stay-at-home mom, and Keith recently opened his own commercial land-scape company.

This is Carole's story:

"What can I tell you? A few weeks ago, Keith talked me into just 'visiting' the puppies at the local pound. Of course, while we were there he said things like, 'Every kid ought to have a dog'; 'If we take one of these pups home today, I'll be in charge of training it'; 'It can stay in the fenced-in backyard 'til I get home every day'; and, 'Sweetheart, you won't have to lift a finger!'

"Keith's a charmer. He just wore me down. And now we've got a barking, drooling, pooping puppy named 'Bozzie' that annoys our neighbors so much we have to keep him indoors!

"I tried to get Keith to train Boz like he said he would, but he says, 'I know I promised to train the dog but that was *before* I landed a big, new landscaping contract. I don't have time to take charge of the dog now; you'll have to.'

"In my more reasonable moments, I understand that Keith can't keep his promise to train the dog. The trouble is I'm angry at him anyway! It's not fair that I'm the one stuck having to deal with Boz. I'm one hundred percent clue-less about pets. Plus, I've already got a full-time job as the mother of our active, demanding little boy. And what's worse, even though I know we can still return the dog to the pound and get our money back—at this point, I'm bouncing back and forth between feeling fond of the dog and resenting Keith for sticking me with the job of having to take care of it!"

Now, see what happens as Carole answers the basic questions:

Question 1:	Answer:	Distracting Thoughts and Worries:
What are my negative feelings? • Pay attention to all your negative feelings. • Toward whom?	**Angry** at Keith for putting me in this position, and I feel **let down** too. **Resentful** that he's not doing what he said he would. **Ashamed** I'm not more understanding about his time constraints. **Sorry for myself. Unsupported. Alone. SCARED.** I'm more **afraid** of having to train the dog than angry at Keith.	I've never had a pet. I'm scared to train one. I don't want to tell Keith I'm frightened. I don't want to sound like a helpless woman who needs her man to handle the tough jobs. Besides, he's under enough pressure at work without having to listen to me.

Question 2:	Answer:	Distracting Thoughts and Worries:
What's the fairest way to describe the problem? • Remove phrases implying you're stuck.	Keith promised I wouldn't have to train the puppy, but now he doesn't have the time to do it himself. ~~I'm the one left to do it and I can't!~~ I don't know how to train a pet.	Scared I'll fail and have to give the dog away or have to live with an untrained pet!

Question 3:	Answer:	Distracting Thoughts and Worries:
Why do I want to work things out? • Focus on positive feelings and/or practical reasons.	Because it'd be easier to let Boz into the house ~~without worrying what he'll do or destroy~~. The neighbors would get some much needed peace and quiet. And I'd be calmer when Keith gets home after work, which would make both of us happier.	It doesn't matter what reasons I have for wanting to work this out—I'm stuck in an impossible situation.

Question 4:	Answer:	Distracting Thoughts and Worries:
How would I like things between us to be?	I'd like us to ~~stop bickering about who's supposed to deal with the dog and just~~ get him trained. Specifically, ~~since he isn't going to do it,~~ I would like Keith to get someone to help me train the dog.	Taking care of the baby and the house and now a dog that's always waking the baby, annoying the neighbors, and making me jumpy— is too much. It's not fair.
• Turn what you **don't** want into what you **do** want.		
• Specify your partner's realistic actions.		

Question 5:	Answer:	Distracting Thoughts and Worries:
How can I actually get that?	Stop waiting for Keith to rescue me. Start handling things myself. Want this finished before next month when his folks come to visit for a week.	
• When, where, under what circumstances?	Take Boz back to the pound? If they can't find him a new owner, they'll put him to sleep. I can't let that happen! Hire a dog trainer? We're on a tight budget; we don't have the money.	I bet Keith's counting on the fact that I can't bring myself to return Boz! The vet probably thinks it's ridiculous to be scared—but I don't care what he thinks, as long as he'll tell me how to train Bozzie.
• Specify your actions.		
• Handle worries.	Ask the vet how to train him? Well, I could at least start with that.	

Question 6:	Answer:	Distracting Thoughts and Worries:
And if that doesn't work, what else can I do? • Specify your actions. • Handle worries. • Keep your goal in mind.	Buy a muzzle so Boz can't bark outside and get Keith to build a doghouse? Even though Keith is really busy, this beats taking Boz to the pound. Trying to live with the fact that they might put him to sleep is out of the question!	I don't have the heart to leave him out in a storm unless he can take shelter. Bozzie's so cute when he plops down at my feet that I'm willing to pester Keith to build him a shelter if that's what it takes.

Outcome

Reading back over her written answers as she moved from one question to the next, Carole was amazed to see how often she'd written the word *scared*:

"I even wrote it down in capital letters. And that word kept popping up in my margin notes too. When I saw that my fear of training the dog was behind my anger at Keith, I still tried not to face that for a while. I think that's because it's easier for me to be angry at someone else and blame him for my unhappiness at how things are than it is to face my own fears. But seeing the word "scared" like that in black and white really did get to me.

"Then a day or so later, just after Keith had left for work one morning, Boz knocked over an entire box of cereal, pooped on the living room rug, startled the baby, and howled at a delivery man. I lost it and burst into tears. When I calmed down, I knew I had to do something about the dog!

"I called the vet and he gave me a few ideas to try. Mostly, what I remember him saying was, 'Relax; dogs are surprisingly tuned-in to their owner's wishes.' I doubted that! When I hung up, I glared at Bozzie, who was sitting at my feet drooling. Then I grabbed an old rag, tossed it to him, and said, 'Keep that in your mouth when you drool!' Boz raced for the rag and kept it in his mouth as he trailed me around the house.

"Eventually, he dropped the rag and started barking. So I picked him up and put him outside. I let him back in five minutes later. He started barking again, and again I put him outside. We went through that drill three times. After that, Boz figured out that when he barked, he'd find himself outside, which he quickly discovered was a great place to poop. By the end of the day, Boz only barked if he needed to go outside or when a stranger approached the house.

"By the time Keith got home, Boz and I were fast friends. I still can't believe that I—someone who's never had a pet in her life—trained that little guy! And to top it all off, when Keith came home and saw what I'd done, he hugged me and gave me the high-five!

"The only problem I have now is that when other people mention how much better-behaved Boz seems to be, Keith tells them when he came home to a well-trained dog he figured I spent the whole day poking Boz in the eye until he did what I wanted him to. Keith thinks that's funny. I don't. It seems to me as if he's making light of what I did, and that hurts. Although now I think I have another reason to ask those six questions of yours."

Observations

Sometimes what looks like or even feels like a relationship problem is something else. Carole learned that when she took the time to answer Question 1 (*What are my negative feelings?*) as thoroughly as she could. Reading over what she'd written, "I'm more *afraid* of having to train the dog than angry at Keith," showed her that underneath (and fueling) her wrath at Keith was something else—her very real fear of training a dog. Once she understood that, she was able to take steps to solve the problem on her own.

Seeing that truth laid out in black in white, not only lessened Carole's anger, it gave her a more accurate view of her problem, and it directed her attention toward the specific and do-able steps that could (and did) lead to a satisfying end result. We believe that Carole's experience makes a strong case for taking the time to fully answer Question 1 by unearthing and adding into your answer the subtle and often difficult-to-acknowledge negative feelings you're bound to have when you find yourself caught up in a conflict with your partner.

He Smokes. She Smolders.

Although only in his mid-fifties, Al had suffered two heart attacks in the past seven years. That he continued to chain-smoke made his wife, Rena, livid. Here is what she told us:

"After his first heart attack, Al was really shaken up and he did everything the doctor told him to do. He ate right, worked out, lost weight, and stopped smoking. He saw the light, but the bulb burned out, and pretty soon he slipped back into his chain-smoking habits.

"After his second heart attack, the doctor spelled it out, saying, 'Either stop smoking or expect to die sooner than you think.' But Al's still puffing away.

"I've tried *everything* to get him to stop. I've screamed, cried, threatened, nagged, and even tried to lay a major guilt trip on him. But he won't quit.

"I can make sure he eats right, and I do. I can drive him to and from the rehab center where they make sure he exercises right. But how can I keep him from killing himself with those damn cigarettes when he flat out refuses to stop smoking?"

Desperate to find out, Rena answered the six questions. As you read her responses, you'll see that we put the coaching cues she found most helpful in parentheses.

Question 1: What are my negative feelings?

Angry at him. *Disgusted* at his lack of willpower. *Frustrated* that I can't make him stop smoking. *Powerless* to get Al to do the right and obvious thing here. Mentally *drained. Hurt* he won't give up smoking for my sake if not for his.

(Pay attention to all your negative feelings.) Terrified of losing him. *Afraid* to live on my own (I've never lived alone. I went from living with my parents to living with a husband). *Helpless* to get him to stop smoking. *Tired* of the battle.

Question 2: What's the fairest way to describe the problem?

The doctor has said that Al needs to stop smoking. His life is at stake. I have begged him to stop smoking for his sake and mine. He refuses. The more I press him, the more he resists me. *(Take out blaming, explaining, or guessing words.)* ~~He's killing himself and doesn't even care how it's hurting me.~~

Question 3: Why do I want to work things out?

So that Al will live longer. So we can be together longer. So he'll start taking care of himself and I can stop being in charge (*Focus on positive feelings and/or practical reasons.*) ~~So that I can stop being so worried about what I'd do without him~~ because I love him so much.

Question 4: How would I like things between us to be?

What I'd like is for the two of us to be so in love and so happy with each other that we would do everything possible to stay healthy. (*Specify your partner's realistic actions.*) Specifically, I would like Al to immediately get into some kind of program to stop smoking. I would like him to do as the doctor recommended: go to the hospital-run stop-smoking classes, try hypnosis or acupuncture to reduce the cravings, and use gum or nicotine patches.

(*What would the perfect partner do?*) First, the perfect partner would tell me he sees how deeply hurt I am by his smoking and that he knows I don't want to lose him. Then he would put his arms around me and assure me that he would stop smoking now no matter how difficult it might be. Once he stopped smoking, we would go back to doing more of the things we enjoy together. We would swim and go for walks together. We would sign up for gardening courses this fall at the university. And Al and I would get back to playing bridge with other couples like we used to before they asked him to leave because they couldn't handle his smoking.

Question 5: How can I actually get that?

I can try asking again and this time do some of the things your book said can help people hang in there and take positive steps to settle their problem, like:

- Jot down my key points on a note card and check off each one as I cover it.
- Minimize distraction by beginning the conversation when and where we won't be disturbed.
- Describe what I hope the outcome of our discussion will be.
- Express my genuine, positive reasons for wanting to work things out.
- Enroll Al by inviting him to suggest how we might solve things together.
- Be prepared to listen.

(*Rehearse blame-free statement.*) Also, I can practice beforehand to make certain my tone of voice isn't angry and my words don't sound accusing. I can wait 'til Wednesday, which is his birthday. He's going to love the gift I got him! I'll give it to him first so he'll be in a really good frame of mind. Then I will kiss him and tell him how dear he is to me and how I want him to be around for many, many years. Then I will show him that I even made some notes to myself because this conversation is so important to me that I am trying to say everything just right. And I will tell him that by the time we finish this conversation what I hope happens is that we feel closer and more loving toward each other than we ever have before. I'll even tell him of my own fears about how I don't want to have to go on living without him and how frightened I am of that prospect.

Question 6: And if that doesn't work, what else can I do?

If I say everything as calmly and as perfectly as I can and he still continues to smoke, then all I can think of to do is go back to nagging him and hiding his cigarettes when I can and things like that. (*Keep your goal in mind.*) That probably won't make him stop smoking, but it is better than doing nothing because if he dies and I haven't at least tried to get him to stop, I couldn't live with the guilt.

(*Handle worries.*) And I can do things to try to fill my days with other people and activities so that I can get ready to live without him. I can call our old bridge group and see if they will let me back in the game as a sub or something. I can send off for a catalogue of the university's upcoming courses and sign up for something on my own. And I can go ahead and join the book club my sister has been asking me to join with her. (*Keep your goal in mind.*) This plan won't give me what I want, but it will take care of some of my fears and it will give me something else to think about besides taking care of Al.

Outcome

Rena telephoned us about a month later to let us know how things had turned out:

"You wouldn't believe how *badly* things went. I had rehearsed over and over. And I had promised myself I'd stay calm and sweet and speak from the heart. And for a few moments, it looked like I actually could pull that off. I took a deep breath, pulled my notes out, and started to tell him all the things I'd planned to say, when all of a sudden all the anger and fear I felt just overpowered my mouth.

"I heard myself yelling at him, 'I can't believe you haven't stopped smoking. I have begged you and I have threatened you and you have even watched me cry myself to sleep over this. Well, Buster, I'm through. You want to smoke yourself to death—you do that. I love you too much to sit around here and watch you kill yourself.'

"Then I grabbed my things and headed for the door. Al came thundering after me asking, 'Where do you think you're going?' And without thinking I hollered back, 'I am going out to prepare myself for your death.'

"Al pulled back as if I had just swung at him. I suddenly worried that I had been too abrupt or too cruel in saying that—maybe it was bad for his heart or something—but my words kept coming. I said that I was tired of being responsible for his life and his health. I said that I wanted him to care about himself and me enough to stop smoking but that I hadn't been able to get him to do that—so now all I could do was take care of myself, and that meant I needed to go out and make new friends and try to figure out how I was going to live without him.

"My uncontrolled outburst got Al's attention in ways that all my nagging, crying, threatening, and pleading hadn't. And for the first time in a while, we started talking—really talking—to each other. I talked about being afraid to live on my own. He talked about being afraid to stop smoking because it was probably too late to do anything that would make a difference in his health.

"After that, Al agreed to try to give up smoking. And I told him—something that was true but unexpected—I said that I hoped he would quit, but I wasn't going to make it my job to see that he did—not any more.

"I didn't end up getting Al to stop smoking. He still sneaks a cigarette every once in a while. I wish he wouldn't. But the bigger change is how I feel about myself now. I am doing more things that bring me satisfaction, and Al is starting to join me—in fact, he sat in for someone at my last bridge game.

"I've really done some thinking about whether answering the six questions helped me or not. I think they did—just not in the way I thought they would.

Answering them made me more aware of my fears about living alone. I think seeing the words I wrote down in my very first answer ('*Afraid* to live on my own. I've never lived alone. I went from living with my parents to living with a husband.') got me thinking about things I could do to make myself feel more involved in my own life instead of only being concerned with my husband's life. I started feeling my own anger at being powerless in this situation and maybe deep down I was tired of trying to be careful around Al and not making things worse. Anyway, answering the questions just brought the truth howling out of me. Then, once I focused on taking charge of myself and not trying to make Al's choices for him, he chose to do a better job of trying to take care of himself."

Observations

In this story, trying to get Al to stop smoking was keeping Rena stuck and feeling powerless. As long as her only objective was to try to change her husband's behavior, Rena's ability to succeed and move forward was out of her control; it was all up to Al.

By asking the basic questions however, Rena was able to notice her own worries, and she began to see that she could take some steps on her own to reduce her sense of powerlessness and some of her fears. That Al ultimately reduced his smoking is a wonderful outcome. However, even if he had not, Rena would have been in a better place having worked through the basic questions.

If you run into a problem and discover that your partner is unwilling to cooperate, finding out as much as you can about your own fears makes it easier and more likely that you will be able to take steps to ease your emotional upheaval and notice the other options you have to get to the best possible positive outcome on your own.

THOUGHTS TO TAKE WITH YOU

When your partner won't budge, it may help you to:
- Hold on to your written answers; you may want to look at them later.
- Focus your action plan on the things your partner will do—rather than on things he or she won't do.

- Pay attention to the feelings in your answer to Question 1 that are not directed toward your partner. They may offer clues about what you can do on your own to settle things.
- Consider creating a back-up plan that does not require your partner to change—but allows for the possibility.

5

Mad about Money

Troubles borrowed, troubles loaned

Ask one hundred people what money means to them, and you get one hundred different answers. For some, money represents peace of mind. For others, it's power, control, or a measure of self-worth. And still others tell us money means exotic excursions, access to top-notch medical care, a college education, financial security during the golden years, a new home, liposuction, the ability to pay off back taxes, or the chance to make larger donations to a favorite charity. No wonder money is a more constant source of discord for couples than almost any other issue!

While financial disputes don't necessarily jeopardize our relationships, when we find ourselves stuck in argument after argument about how money is spent, saved, managed, shared, or withheld, the urge to fight, fold, or flee can overtake us in a flash. The problem with fighting, folding, or fleeing, however, is it seldom (if ever) leads to a long-term happy ending. So what can you do to settle your money differences?

You are about to hear from four people who are struggling over a variety of money problems. These are a wife who's grown weary of justifying every purchase she makes to her husband, a husband who can't bring himself to tell his wife that he lost his job, another husband who takes steps on his own to curb what he believes is his wife's tendency to lend money irresponsibly, and a couple at odds about how to pay off their debt.

Although their problems are distinct and each of their stories leads somewhere different, these people have at least two important things in common:

they'd all like to talk calmly with their spouses about their money conflicts, and at the start, they each believe that discussions about money are so touchy or so potentially explosive that they're unlikely to do much good.

What they discover—and we hope you will too—is that even when negative feelings like anger, fear, worry, resentment, exasperation, and helplessness threaten to derail you, relying on the coaching cues described in chapter 2 as you answer the basic questions makes it possible to calmly address and effectively resolve a wide range of financial disputes with your partner.

The Unequal Sequel

This story captures the dilemma that can accompany a woman's choice to put her career on hold while her children are young. People often measure themselves (and others) in terms of how much wealth they have accumulated or how high their salary is. With most couples, that means there's an imbalance right off the bat. And that certainly was the case for Lisa, a young mother who'd put her own career on hold in order to be a stay-at-home mom. That imbalance produced mounting anger during what she calls her "sequel" years.

One afternoon, Lisa approached us and said, "Just curious about this new book you're working on. Mind if I look?" Then she sat down and leafed through our manuscript. When she came across the words, "Mad about Money," Lisa sucked in her breath, shoved the manuscript hastily back toward us, and sighed, "My husband, Bob, and I fight about money all the time, but we never get anywhere."

We nodded and said, "Sounds exhausting. What's going on?"

"Oh, you know—the bills come, Bob sits down to pay them, and all of a sudden he starts saying things like, 'Did you really spend a hundred and fifty-two dollars for *that?*' or, 'Look at all these bills and *not one* of these charges is mine!' And that's all it takes. My heart starts pounding a mile a minute, and I bounce back and forth between being frightened and getting mad!"

"Then, what do you do?" we asked.

"Depends. Sometimes I explain what each item is. I tell him how I really shopped around and didn't buy a single thing, 'til I made sure I'd gotten it at the lowest price. Other times I answer him in an angry way, and then he'll say,

'Hey, what are you making such a big deal about? I just want to make sure we're paying the right amount!' That gets me all confused and embarrassed.

"I'm never sure whether he's accusing me of spending too much money, or if he just wants to make sure the bill is correct. But either way, I feel accused of something. And it's awful to have to explain every damn thing I buy!

"I used to have a great job. That was in the first part of our marriage. Back then," she smiled, "I made more money than Bob, so I could buy things whenever I wanted without having these kinds of fights. But when the kids were born, I wanted to be a full-time mom. Bob wanted that too.

"Now I'm stuck living in the sequel to those first years of marriage. But hey, Bob's business is doing fine, so we can afford to live on what he makes. And so far it's working."

"Doesn't sound like it's working too well for you," we told her quietly.

"No, I guess it isn't," she admitted with a sad shrug. "But that's how things are. What can you do?"

"You could try answering the six basic questions. To help you get the most from each of your answers, we'll coach you along the way," we told her.

"I'll try anything if you tell me that it'll work!"

"How about we let you tell *us* that after you've tried our approach," we responded.

Here is what Lisa wrote as we talked her through the questions:

Question 1:	Lisa's Initial Answer:	Distracting Thoughts and Worries:
What are my negative feelings?	Right now I'm just **angry**. **Angry at Bob** for acting as if I'm accountable to him if I even buy a stick of gum! **Angry at myself** for not making it clear that this is not what I signed on for when I said "I do." And I'm even **unreasonably mad at the kids** because having them means it's impossible for me to go out and earn my own money for the next seven or eight years!	

"Pretty good answer," we told Lisa. "But when you're upset about a predictable, recurring problem like the upheaval you experience when it's time to pay bills, it's a good idea to think about the full range of your negative feelings. Pay attention to all your negative feelings. Go beyond your obvious feelings of anger. Look for other subtle and more difficult-to-acknowledge feelings."

Then we suggested that Lisa try asking herself, "What negative feelings get triggered in me whenever I'm in this kind of situation?" When you can remember and list the negative feelings that have surged through you before, it's easier to figure out how to keep them from overtaking you the next time you're caught up in a similar situation.

Here is Lisa's more constructive answer:

Question 1:	Lisa's More Constructive Answer:	Distracting Thoughts and Worries:
What are my negative feelings? • Toward whom? • Pay attention to all your negative feelings.	It depends. Sometimes I get **angry at Bob**. Sometimes I feel **ashamed of myself** for being afraid to stand up for myself. And sometimes I **hate myself** for blaming the kids for any of this. Mostly, I'm **afraid** to spend a dime on anything that's not essential. And I get **resentful** when I get called on the carpet to explain my purchases to Bob as if I'm an irresponsible, money-wasting woman. The worst part is that I get **nervous** when I know the bills are about to arrive.	

When she finished, we moved on to the next question:

Question 2:	Lisa's Initial Answer:	Distracting Thoughts and Worries:
What's the fairest way to describe the problem?	Bob's a control freak who watches every dollar. I'm not making any money right now, so I'm forced to spend his.	

We told Lisa it was important to get rid of negative labels that show up in your answer. Describing Bob as a "control freak" is one of those critical labels that keep people focused on who's right and who's wrong instead of answering Question 2 by describing the problem as a difference in personalities, styles, or priorities.

To help her answer this question more objectively, we also suggested she use the phrase "We are different when it comes to...." And, we told her that if she still had trouble coming up with an objective statement of the problem, she might try asking herself, "What do we usually do when this issue crops up?" This simply calls for a straightforward description of the actions you both take. It does not leave room for you to assume or conclude that the way you and your spouse react is the only option either of you have.

Finally, we pointed out that her words, *I'm forced to* suggest that she sees herself as powerless to improve things. That's a belief that can really leave you stuck.

When phrases like *I'm forced to* or *there's nothing I can do* or *he'll never change* show up in your answer, it's best to notice and remove those words or drop them into the margin. Doing that will make it less likely that you'll get hung up thinking about what you *can't* do instead of focusing on what you *can* do.

Lisa nodded and reworded her answer:

Question 2:	Lisa's More Constructive Answer:	Distracting Thoughts and Worries:
What's the fairest way to describe the problem? • We are different. • No blaming, explaining, or guessing. • Remove phrases implying you're stuck. • What do we usually do?	We're different when it comes to paying bills. Bob handles things like an accountant. He usually asks me about the items I've charged. Then, I usually feel like he doesn't trust me. I get angry and we end up fighting.	Bob watches where every dollar he makes goes. I'm not making money right now so I'm forced to spend his.

Lisa told us that when she'd asked herself, "What do we usually do when this crops up?" she found it easier to answer Question 2. She said, "That way, I could describe how we are different when it comes to paying the bills—and I could do that without blaming Bob as I was writing my answer."

Question 3:	Lisa's Initial Answer:	Distracting Thoughts and Worries:
Why do I want to work things out?	I want to work this out because having my own money, which would resolve the problem, isn't going to happen for at least seven years. And I'm tired of having this happen every month!	

We smiled and told Lisa we thought she'd answered Question 3 perfectly by putting into words her practical reason for wanting to settle the problem. We explained that sometimes people pull up their warm and tender reasons for wanting to work things out. Other times, they focus on practical, pragmatic reasons like Lisa did. Either way, answering this question strengthens your resolve to work through a dispute and increases your willingness to hang in there when the going gets tough.

Lisa's initial answer seemed so complete that there was no reason for her to tackle the question a second time. So we moved on to the next question.

Question 4:	Lisa's Initial Answer:	Distracting Thoughts and Worries:
How would I like things between us to be?	I'd like Bob to trust that I'm as committed to keeping our heads above water as he is and to stop hassling me! I have no idea what he could do differently because he's so set in his ways.	His father paid bills the same way. As far as I can tell, his mother had no problem with that. So Bob thinks **I'm wrong** and that I'm making a moun-tain out of a molehill.

Noting that Lisa's answer was nice sounding but nonspecific ("trust that I'm as committed…as he is"), that it centered around what she didn't want ("stop hassling me") instead of what she did want, and that she didn't specify the steps she'd like Bob to take ("I have no idea what he could do…") we gave her the coaching cues to the left of her answer below:

Question 4:	Lisa's More Constructive Answer:	Distracting Thoughts and Worries:
How would I like things between us to be? • Specify your partner's realistic actions. • What would the perfect partner do? • Turn what you **don't** want into what you **do** want.	I'd like us to be equal partners when it comes to managing our money and for us to be able to talk about the bills calmly and with respect. The perfect husband would come home from work, kiss me hello, and say that after the kids go to bed, he planned to pay some bills. He'd say, "I'll read the kids their story tonight and give you a chance to look over the bills before I pay them. If anything looks incorrect, circle it and we'll talk about it when I finish. If things look fine to you, I'll pay the bills as they are, OK?"	

Lisa smiled. She seemed relaxed until we asked her the next question:

Question 5:	Lisa's Initial Answer:	Distracting Thoughts and Worries:
How can I actually get that?	You tell me! Bob would **never** handle bill paying that way. It wouldn't even occur to him!	

Clearly reluctant to answer this question, Lisa fidgeted and chewed her pencil. So we asked her to drop into the margin every reason she could think of to support her belief that nothing she could do would improve things.

We explained that *dropping her worries into the margin would help her notice her negative thoughts and feelings without letting them get in her way.* We also explained that when you begin formulating a plan to help you get what you'd really like, new worries tend to pop up and feed your belief that nothing you can do will work.

We suggested she drop her newest worries in the margin and then ask herself, "Taking all of my objections into account, how can I get what I'd like?"

Lisa nodded, but insisted, "Bob isn't ever going to say those kinds of things to me before he sits down to pay bills unless…"

Question 5:	Lisa's More Constructive Answer:	Distracting Thoughts and Worries:
How can I actually get that? • When, where, under what circumstances? • Specify your actions. • Keep your goal in mind. • Rehearse blame-free statement. • Handle worries.	Unless I write a script and tell him to read his part before he sits down to pay the bills next month! Which I guess I could. Bob says he **never** knows what to expect from me. And he likes that I'm not a boring person. Bob says I keep him on his toes. So giving him a script would fit right into that. Still, the only way around my worries is for me to have two different scripts for Bob. One for how I want him to talk to me if he comes home in a bad mood and another one if he seems calm. Both scripts would have to end with Bob saying something like, "I trust you	If he's had a bad day, there's no way he'll try this. He's too much of a control freak to go along with this.

Question 5: (cont.)	Lisa's More Constructive Answer: Lisa. I know that you spend money cautiously, and if there is no circled item on the bill, I promise I won't give you a hard time about what you've spent."	Distracting Thoughts and Worries:

When she'd finished Question 5, Lisa threw her hands up in the air and said, "Even if Bob is in a good mood, even if he goes along with this idea, and even if every single item on every single bill is correct, he still might challenge me, and then we'd end up fighting again!"

Question 6: And if that doesn't work, what else can I do?	Lisa's Initial Answer: I have no idea what to do if that doesn't work. And I really don't think it will work.	Distracting Thoughts and Worries:

Because Lisa was too worried about what could go wrong to develop a constructive answer to this question, we asked, "Suppose your first plan does meet with failure, what will you do? Think about it. What will you say to Bob if he won't go along with your script idea? Try describing in detail *the specific and do-able steps you will take to reopen the discussion with him.*

"If you continue having trouble answering this question, *drop your worries in the margin and come up with a plan that includes the specific steps you will take to handle those worries.* Write out your answer again. Be sure to include a realistic time, place, and circumstance to put your back-up plan into motion."

Question 6:	Lisa's More Constructive Answer:	Distracting Thoughts and Worries:
And if that doesn't work, what else can I do? • When, where, under what circumstances? • Specify your actions. • Handle worries. • Rehearse again.	If he refuses to read the script or challenges me afterwards, then I will tell him I want us to agree on a set amount of money I can spend each month. I'll sit down with him right then and stay put until we've come up with an amount that seems reasonable to both of us. Then I'll ask for his written promise (I'll make out a contract in advance for him to sign) to look **only** at the total amount I spend each month with the understanding that as long as it falls within the agreed upon amount, he won't ask me to explain **any** item.	I'm worried he still might challenge me, and then we'd end up fighting again.

After she'd answered Question 6, Lisa sat quietly lost in thought until she glanced at her watch, jumped up, and said, "Uh-oh, I've got to run if I'm going to make it to my daughter's basketball game. Thanks for your help. I'll let you know what happens."

And the very next day, she did that.

Outcome

"Oh good," she said as she rushed over to us. "I wasn't sure you'd be here this early. I've got something amazing to tell you! Bob left work early yesterday and turned up at our daughter, Sarah's, basketball game on time to watch the last fifteen minutes. When it was over, both kids went with Sarah's coach to watch another team. Bob and I decided we'd go get a bite and meet them over there.

"Then came the worst question in the world—the one that goes, 'Where do you want to eat?' Sounded to me like a setup—you know, where if I pick a place he thinks is too expensive, he looks at me as if to say—'there you go again, spending money we don't have.' So I snapped at him and said—'It's *your* dollar. You decide where you want to spend it!'

"Bob frowned and said, 'What are you talking about? It's *not* just my money any more than the kids are just *your* children!'

"'Well you could've fooled me,' I hissed at him. 'You're always picking on me about what I spend, always trying to get me to cut back as if it *is* just your money.'

"'You gotta be kidding me,' he shouted.

"'No, I'm not kidding,' I hollered back. 'And I'm finished having this same fight. Why can't we act like people who love and trust each other instead of people who go for each other's throats whenever it's time to spend a damn dollar?'

"'Fine—you want us to be different people? You go first,' he yelled.

"And I said, 'Fine. Give me five minutes and I will!'

"I tore a piece of paper from one of the kid's notepads, went to the ladies room, and sat in a stall writing a few sentences. I brought my piece of paper over to Bob who was pacing up and down in front of his car waiting.

"'Read this,' I said. 'I want you to say your lines and I'll say mine. Ready?'

"'I'm not in the mood for games, Lisa,' he snarled.

"'Neither am I! This isn't a game. You don't want to read it? Fine, I'll read both parts—all you have to do is listen.'

"Then I went ahead and read his lines in a booming fake voice and mine in a soft, sweet one:

Bob: Lisa my wonderful wife, I've only got about fifteen dollars in cash on me right now, can you think of a place to go where that'll cover our dinner and tip?

Me: Why yes, dear Bob, who works so hard to support our family and who managed to show up at Sarah's basketball game anyway, how about that soup and salad place down the block?

Bob: Good idea my love, let's go check that place out.

Me: You know, honey, I've got six dollars and some change with me—we can use that too, if it helps.

Bob: Thanks, it might. Now let's go and enjoy our first meal in ages away from the kids.

"I finished and made one of those big sweeping bows like people do at the end of a play and Bob clapped. Then we hugged each other and went out for a nice, simple dinner. He asked how I'd thought of writing a script to get us to stop fighting, and I said, 'It just sort of came to me over a cup of coffee.'

"I also said I was going to present him with another script shortly.

"'How shortly?' he asked.

"'In about four weeks, right before you sit down to pay the bills next month,' I said.

"Bob nodded and said, 'Maybe by then I'll be ready to read my own lines.'

"I laughed and said, 'Well my dear, darling husband—there's plenty of room for you up here onstage with me.'"

Observations

Much like what happened for Scott in chapter 2, Lisa's concrete plan gave way to a spontaneous, creative solution in which she found a way to use her script idea—at a time, in a place, and under circumstances far removed from their bill paying conflict. Whenever we can address our relationship struggles in a setting outside the problem, we tend to act more calmly and our partners tend to be more receptive to our concerns and requests.

What She Doesn't Know

Although we met the man in this story by chance, we intentionally included his experience here in order to help you overcome any hesitation you may feel about the value of inviting a counseling professional to help you and your partner begin addressing the issues that divide you.

This is the account of a man in his mid-forties who sat slumped over a stack of newspaper "help wanted" ads, ignoring his coffee. Every once in a while, he circled an item with a thick black marker. The rest of the time he sighed, rattled newspaper pages, and muttered in our general direction.

"Nothing! Nothing at all in these want ads," he said in disgust. "All they've got are jobs I'm too old to do—or jobs I'm not qualified for. You work for a company for years and one day—boom!—the place folds and you're out of work. What am I going to do when my unemployment benefits run out? I've just got a few weeks left. How's Cindy going to take this?"

Thinking that he was speaking to us, we asked, "Who's Cindy?"

"Cindy? Oh, sorry, I didn't know I was talking out loud!"

"No problem. But you sound upset, are you all right?" we asked.

"Yeah, I'm okay. Just having trouble finding work. Cindy's my wife. I'm so worried about her I must've been thinking out loud. My name's Doug, by the way."

"Is your wife having a tough time holding it together while you look for work?"

"Well, you see—I haven't exactly told her. I mean she's so high strung and last year she went through a pretty scary thing. Found out she had cancer, then a real rough series of surgeries. So, I'm trying not to worry her. I mean the doctor says she has to avoid stress. I've been thinking that I'd get another job before I say anything," he finished lamely.

"Where does she think you go everyday?"

"I just let her think I'm at work—same as always."

"What'll you do if she finds out the company you used to work for folded?"

"That *can't* happen! I won't let it!"

"Well, but have you thought about sitting down and talking to her about this?" we asked him.

"Yeah, I've thought about it. Lately that's all I think about. But I've waited too long. She's going to be furious with me for not telling her right away. She'll call me a liar and a lot of other things. And she'll be worried about money—terrified, actually, because this fall we'll have both our boys in college and the bill for that is a big one. Then she'll start saying we have to sell the house or that she's got to go back to work full time. Cindy works a few days a week in a hospital gift shop. I'm afraid she'll get so frantic she'll make herself sick!

"I can't take that chance. So, I'm just going to avoid telling her for another week and keep pounding the pavement looking for a job that gives me decent health benefits. That's the key thing for us—we've got to have insurance.

"Well, enough about me," he said, suddenly looking embarrassed. "Are you two writing a book?"

"Yes. We're getting ready to send a rough draft of it out. Would you like to read some it?"

"Yeah, sure, I've finished the want ads for today, and I can't go home for a few more hours. Hand it over."

We noticed that Doug was writing something as he read, but we were hard at work and thought he was probably making notes to himself about job leads or something. A while later, Doug handed the book back to us, mumbled something about it being interesting reading, and drove off.

We didn't see Doug again but we did get an email from him. (It seems he copied our email address from the cover of our manuscript.)

This is a portion of Doug's email:

I don't know if you'll remember me. We talked about how to tell my wife I was out of work, and you let me read your book. It really helped me, and I wanted you to know that. If you want to know the details you can telephone me. My number's at the bottom of this message.

Sincerely, Doug

P.S. Let me know when your book is finished so I can get a copy and read the whole thing.

We were curious to know what Doug had gotten from his quick read of our book, so we phoned him, and here's what he said:

"While I was reading, I made a list of the basic questions and put the list in my pocket. I looked at it for a few days. Then I decided to write down my own answers to the questions. I thought, how hard can it be to answer six questions? Well, it wasn't really that hard, but it got complicated. Let me read you what I wrote:

"Question 1: *Angry* I'm in this mess, *scared* to tell Cindy, *worried* about paying two college tuitions.

"Question 2: I got laid off and didn't tell Cindy. I wanted to wait until I got another job. Still don't have one. Benefits about to run out. Have to tell her soon.

"Question 3: Cindy and the boys need health insurance and money.

"Question 4: I'd like the two of us to figure some way out of this mess. I'd like Cindy to listen to me calmly. I want her to understand why I waited and to forgive me for not telling her sooner.

"Question 5: Call her doctor, ask how stress affects her health and if there's a good way to give her bad news without compromising her health.

"Question 6: Maybe finally go with her to church and sort of set it up so that the minister she likes can sit down with us while I tell her."

Outcome

"Calling her doctor was a bust! All he did was lecture me about how it was often much worse for a patient's health to keep a secret from them than to tell the truth. So the only other thing I could think of was to check out the minister Cindy likes. I think I shocked her by going to church with her that week.

"After the service, I hung back and reintroduced myself to Reverend Mathews. I didn't tell him what was going on, but I asked him if he ever met privately with his parishioners. He said he did and that he'd be happy to meet with me if I'd like.

"I called him the next day and we got together for about forty-five minutes a few days later. When I explained my problem, he was pretty decent about it. He didn't act like I was a loser damned to burn in Hell or anything. But he did say it was time for me to share this burden with Cindy. I said, 'I know, but how?'

"He said if I wanted to come in with Cindy the next evening, he'd try to help us both deal with the truth together.

"When I got home, I told Cindy I'd spoken to Reverend Mathews about some of the stress I'd been feeling lately and that he had suggested we come in and talk with him together. Cindy looked surprised, but she didn't ask any questions.

"We went the next night, and Cindy took the news about my being out of work pretty hard. I was glad the minister was there. He helped us talk about our feelings for a while. Then he gave us some straight talk about telling the boys together, which we did.

"Right now, although we're doing the best we can, money is still a problem. Cindy picked up a few more hours at the hospital, enough to qualify for health coverage. I got part-time work with a landscaper. The boys applied for student loans, and we're hoping that'll come through.

"Your book didn't solve my money problems, but it helped me figure out how to solve my marriage problem. I don't think I could've done that unless I'd had your six questions."

Observations

When a relationship problem seems too big or feels too risky to tackle alone, involving an experienced professional in your discussions can make it a great deal easier for you to move forward with your partner.

In this case, Doug engaged the help of his minister, a man that he felt he could trust and someone he knew his wife liked. Of course, not every problem requires a therapist. But keep in mind that involving a trained and trusted third person in your problem-solving efforts is always an option. Sometimes it's the best option.

Say "Uncle"

Here is another example of how to move forward when your partner will not cooperate:

"This is not your usual story about money problems," Lowell insisted. "Margie and I live quite comfortably. We're lucky in that regard. Our problem— well, *my* problem, anyway, is what we do with our money. Margie thinks it's just fine to give it away! A con artist comes along with a good sob story and the next thing you know she's giving money to people she knows nothing about. I finally got her to stop doing that—well, I thought I had.

"But I didn't count on her free-loading Uncle Ray. She gave him an enormous amount of money, and when I found out, she said, 'I didn't *give* him the money. It's a loan. He'll pay us back.'

"Well, I got Uncle Ray on the phone and told him I expected him to sign a formal loan agreement and start paying us back immediately. Good old Uncle Ray signed the promissory note all right, and he paid us the agreed-upon amount for about eight months. Then, no big surprise—the payments stopped! I'm ready to take legal action, but Margie says if I do, she'll leave me!

"It's not just that we're out a huge amount of money—although that's certainly part of the problem—it's also the principle of the thing to me. I hate deadbeats, and I'm furious with Margie for getting us involved with one.

"I've tried reasoning with her. I don't want to lose her. I can't imagine living without her. But this is a lot of money we're talking about.

"The kids have talked to her. So have my lawyers. Nobody can convince her that we have to take legal action. I don't imagine this is the kind of problem your book deals with, is it?"

"It's a new one for sure," we admitted. "But the six questions might be able to help you anyway, if you're interested in trying them."

Lowell looked surprised and said he doubted our approach could help him since he, his lawyers, and the kids had all hit a brick wall. We simply smiled and remained quiet. Finally, Lowell scratched his head, sighed, and with obvious misgivings said, "What the heck, I'll try it."

Here are his answers:

Question 1: What are my negative feelings?

I'm *angry* at Margie and *frustrated* at not being able to get through to her. I'm really *afraid* she might leave me over this. And I'm *furious* with her uncle. I always thought he was smarmy, but this is way beyond smarmy. This is exploitation!

Question 2: What's the fairest way to describe this problem?

Margie loaned her uncle a lot of money. He's obligated to pay us back and he hasn't. I want to take legal action against him. Margie says you do not sue family. She says if I do, she'll leave me. I don't want to lose her over this, but it's too much money to just shake my head and forget about.

Question 3: Why do I want to work things out?

I love my wife; I don't want to lose her, and I don't want to kiss all that money goodbye.

Question 4: How would I like things between us to be?

I'd like to be able to talk to Margie about this without her giving me an ultimatum. There's got to be some middle ground here where we can do something to get the money back. You know, what I'd really like is for us to be the kind of couple who, if a family member needs help, sits down together and comes up with the best way to help them so we don't end up in this kind of a jam.

Question 5: How can I actually get that?

I've already tried every way I know of to reason with Margie *and* to get our money back. At this point, I'm afraid the only thing I can do is give in—drop my case against Ray and tell Margie I'd rather have her than the money. But if I do that, I'm damn sure going to keep this from happening again. I'll have to get Margie to promise me that.

Question 6: And if that doesn't work, what else can I do?

If Margie won't promise never to do this sort of thing again, I'll go down to the bank myself and switch things around so that she can't get her hands on large sums of our money without my knowledge. I'm going to limit our vulnerability no matter what!

Outcome

Lowell told us he went home, took Margie's hands in his, and told her he'd spent the whole day worried about what to do. He said he loved her and that while he hoped she wouldn't make him choose between staying married to her and the safety of their financial future, if she did, he'd choose her.

"Margie said she loved me too and that she was sorry for creating this mess. I was all set to make her promise she'd never put us in this kind of financially risky position again when she threw herself into my arms and sobbed with such intensity and relief that I never got a chance to say that. And I'm glad I didn't because when Margie stopped crying, she quietly told me why her Uncle Ray needed the money and why he's so important to her.

"I'm not going to tell you what she said—that's private, family business. But I will say this—Margie and I are back on track and I believe we're going to stay that way now.

"I stopped being so set on suing Ray, and that's when I remembered a suggestion that one of the lawyers had made. If I hadn't calmed down, I might not have picked up on his suggestion that we take out a life-insurance policy on Ray in the amount that he owes and name ourselves and the children as the bene-ficiaries. That way, Ray can have the money now, and eventually we or the kids will get the money back—minus the cost of the policy, of course. So, that's how things worked out. Those six questions of yours actually helped. Thanks."

Observations

In chapter 2 we talked about the role that tone-of-voice plays in communicat-ing with your partner. We think that Lowell's story demonstrates how impor-tant a factor tone-of-voice really is. As he answered each of the six questions, Lowell became clearer about how dear Margie was to him and how much he didn't want to lose her. Those emotions were so present in him that he opened his discussion with Margie with an expression of his genuine tender and loving feelings for her. We believe that his tone of voice in that moment—more than anything else—set the tone for all that followed.

Peanut Butter and Piggy Banks

Phyllis, a former patient of Paul's, who'd been married for just a few years, allowed us to share her story here. Some time ago, she arrived for her session with Paul obviously distraught.

"I'm so mad at my husband I could spit nails right at his stupid, grinning face!" Phyllis exploded.

"Want to tell me what's going on?"

"It's the same old thing—M-O-N-E-Y. But now it's worse! After his mom got sick and we had to put her in the hospital for seven months, we got strapped with so many bills that we're barely making ends meet. And we're *both* sup-posed to cut back on what we spend until we pay off those bills. We made a deal and I've kept it, but yesterday I found out Fred's a lying, little sneak!"

"Fred's a lying, little sneak?"

"That's right! He got a new credit card—just in his name so I wouldn't know he's been going out to fancy lunches with the guys at work. I'll bet he's eating fifteen-dollar steaks while I'm at work eating peanut butter sandwiches that I brought from home. What's the matter with him? Can't he exercise a *little* restraint? I mean, we have all these things we hope to be able to do as soon as we get out from under this debt, and maybe that'll never happen because I'm married to a spoiled, sneaky child instead of a grown man! What am I going to do?" she wailed.

Paul sat quietly for a few moments and then said, "It seems to me there are a couple of different ways we could tackle this. I'm not sure which one would be most helpful for you, so I'm inclined to have you decide. We can spend this time exploring your feelings, giving you a safe place to vent, and looking back at some past experiences you've had that might be fueling your feelings. Or we could try doing something that will focus your attention on finding ways to help you settle things with Fred. Which one sounds like it would be most helpful to you?"

"I'm tired of looking at where I've been. And I'm tired of living with things the way they are. So let's talk about finding ways to settle this," Phyllis replied.

Paul nodded. Then he explained the six basic questions and gave Phyllis some of the same coaching cues that we presented in chapter 2 to help her stay on track when her anger and worries threatened to overwhelm her. As you read Phyllis's written responses, you'll see that she answered Questions 1 through 4 and 6 quickly. She spent more time writing out her answer to Question 5 (*How can I actually get that?*) where she played out in her mind *what* she would do, *why* she would do things that way, and even came up with an interesting way to turn her desire to "rattle" her husband into a good reason for staying calm.

Question 1: What are my negative feelings?

Angry at Fred and *distrustful* of him. *Scared* about the future. *Worried* Fred will act irresponsibly about money and we'll be poor.

Question 2: What's the fairest way to describe this problem?

We made a deal to cut back anywhere we could to pay down the bills. I kept the deal. Fred went behind my back and broke it. I'm angry.

Question 3: Why do I want to work things out?

Want to trust my husband. Want to get this debt off our backs. Want to save money for vacations, a new car, and maybe a baby.

Question 4: How would I like things between us to be?

I'd like us to have a plan we'll both follow without having to police each other that will help us be debt-free and save enough money to start a family.

Question 5: How can I actually get that?

Tonight, ask Fred how we can pay bills and save money without him feeling like he has to sneak around to go out for lunch with the guys at work and without me having to eat peanut butter sandwiches everyday. Last time we talked, I said we should cut back everywhere we could to pay off our bills.

This time, I'm going to wait 'til Fred comes up with his own idea. If he thinks of a plan, then he'll probably follow it—and that's the most important thing! Staying calm will probably rattle him because he's so used to me yelling when I'm mad. Fred will probably wonder when the next shoe's going to drop. And I do want to rattle him!

The more I think about how *not* yelling will get to him, the easier it'll be for me to keep calm. And being calm is the only way I can ever get Fred to hear me anyway.

Question 6: And if that doesn't work, what else can I do?

Go to one of those consumer credit-counselor places together?

Outcome

At her next session, Phyllis smiled at Paul and said, "I did it. I stayed really calm, and Fred admitted he wanted to spend money without having to get my approval. He suggested that each month we both get a set amount to spend, no questions asked.

"Fred might still eat out with the guys at work. I'm still bringing my lunch to work because I'd rather get a manicure every week than eat out.

"Now that we have a new plan to get the bills paid, we're starting to think about trying to get pregnant next year. After we talked, Fred brought home three goofy-looking piggy banks. One is a miniature house; one is a small, red sports car, and the other one's a smiley-faced pregnant woman. Each night, we put whatever change we have in the piggy bank of our choice. This morning I held the sports-car piggy bank and shook it hard. I figured since Fred's always wanted a red Porsche, he'd have thrown his change into that bank. But I was wrong, as I discovered when I shook the pregnant woman piggy bank. It was so full, I almost cried with joy!"

Observations

This story makes two important points. First, after calmly describing the specific relationship problem you have with your partner, and before you move on to make a request, you may want to allow the silence to grow. Doing so can give your partner time to consider your words, identify his or her feelings, and perhaps come up with a good solution you might not have thought of on your own.

Second, while there may be times when your partner will not cooperate, the benefits of fostering the possibility that he or she might cannot be overstated.

We think Phyllis put it best when she said, "Last time we talked about the bills, I'm the one who came up with the idea of cutting back everywhere we could to pay them off. This time, I'm going to be quiet no matter what and wait 'til Fred comes up with his own idea. If he's the one who thinks of it, then he'll probably follow it, and that's the most important thing."

Thoughts to Take with You

To calmly and effectively resolve your financial disputes it can be helpful to:

- Discuss it at a time, in a place, and under circumstances outside your dispute.
- Invite a trusted third person into the problem-solving discussion.
- Be aware that your tone of voice in the moment can be as or even more important than the words you use.
- Seek your partner's ideas about a solution.

6

Behaviors That Hurt, Embarrass, Upset, or Offend

When a partner's actions strike you as selfish, dismissive, rude, or worse

In this chapter we turn the intensity up and look at stories from those who view themselves as "victims" of their spouse's objectionable behavior. Here, four people describe how they dealt with a partner's inappropriate touching, disturbing Internet chat activities, public put downs, and refusals to attend family functions. All of these people participated in a workshop about what to do when you can't get through to your mate.

Even as they struggled with unpleasant behaviors and uncooperative spouses, these individuals chose not to be punishing, manipulative, or vengeful. Instead, using their answers to the six basic questions as a guide, they looked for and took the high road out of their difficulties. We think their stories represent the remarkably upbeat outcomes people can achieve when they concentrate on changing how they respond to objectionable behavior rather than on trying to change the way someone else behaves.

As you read along, keep in mind that whether or not the solutions these people came up with appeal to you, what matters is that each person found an effective way to change, repair, and improve their relationship when all the talking, explaining, begging, complaining, and demanding in the world seemed not to be enough.

How to Handle a Goose

Carla, a woman who'd been married for nearly fifteen years, was embarrassed and horrified by her husband's behavior. Her story shows that it really is possible to settle a relationship problem even when one partner seems steadfastly unwilling to cooperate. Carla describes her situation as follows:

"When John and I got married, he started doing something that really upset me. Every now and then he would poke at my breasts or goose (grab) me in the crotch. I never liked it, but I didn't say anything because he didn't do it that often.

"In the beginning, I tried to accept it as his way of showing affection. But now he's doing it more and more, even in public. I hate it, and I can't get him to see that it's wrong! If I push his hands away, he just winks and grins at me as if to say, 'Aren't I cute?' John is mature about a lot of things. But when it comes to this, he acts like a horny, immature teenager.

"Part of the problem is that his dad does the same thing to his mom, even when other people are around. And then they all just laugh their heads off about it—his mom included. I've tried to laugh it off too, but I just can't.

"It isn't that I don't appreciate John's playfulness, but the *way* he grabs at me embarrasses me to death! I've tried to get him to stop doing this. I've tried shaking my head, pulling away from him, and talking 'til I'm blue in face and he still doesn't get that it really upsets me.

"At this point, I'm through explaining how I feel. He'll never get it, so why bother? I'm trying not to care anymore. I've even started pulling away from him sexually, which is a shame because our sex life used to be so good. It seems to me that if John really loved and respected me, he'd have stopped grabbing at me long ago."

As you watch Carla work her way through the basic questions, you will notice that, except for crossing out a few blaming words, she had no trouble answering Questions 1 through 3.

Question 1: What are my negative feelings?

When we're with other people, I'm *tense*—I feel like I'm waiting for the other shoe to drop. *Worried* that John's going to grab at me and thoroughly *embarrassed* when he does. But when I'm by myself and thinking about this—I feel *angry, humiliated,* and *unloved.*

Question 2: What is the fairest way to describe the problem?

We are different when it comes to how John should touch me when people are around. He grabs at me or gooses me and says he's "just being playful." I don't like it and I want him to stop doing that. So far, he hasn't stopped.

Question 3: Why do I want to work things out?

So I'll feel more affectionate toward my husband. And so that ~~instead of being wary all the time—afraid he's going to do something that embarrasses me at any moment,~~ I can relax and enjoy myself when we are out with other people.

Question 4: How would I like things between us to be?

All I want is for my husband to stop goosing me in public. That's it!

Rereading what she'd written, Carla realized she'd put into words what she *didn't* want instead of what she *did* want. So she reworded her answer as we suggest in chapter two by replacing what you *don't* want with a direct statement about what you *do* want.

Here is her more positive response:

Question 4: How would I like things between us to be?

I would like us to be affectionate in public without being sexual or suggestive.

Question 5: How can I actually get that?

How can I get John to stop grabbing at me? I can't!!!!!!

Carla said she couldn't think of a way to answer Question 5 because she'd already tried (and failed at) every idea she had. We assured her this was a common first reaction to this question—especially for people who've tried many times and in many ways to persuade their partners to change upsetting behaviors.

We explained, "Even when you're convinced you've already done all you can to improve things, it's important to identify at least one practical step you've not yet taken."

To help Carla generate ideas, we asked her to try one of the fill-in-the-blank statements that accompany the brain-storm-when-you're-stuck coaching cue (see chapter 2).

She liked the one about jotting down every thing she'd already done, noticing what was not on her list, and turning one of those things into a full blown answer to the question. Here's how she proceeded: First, she made a list of the things she'd already tried (see below):

I've already tried talking, yelling, shoving his hands away, crying, not speaking to him, showing him stories from newspaper columnists who agree with me and nothing—I mean NOTHING—makes any difference.

After reviewing the above, Carla generated this list of things she hadn't yet tried:

I haven't gone out and bought armored clothing to wear as protection from goosing.

I haven't tried staying home or refusing to go anywhere in public with him.

I haven't made a public scene when he grabs for me.

I haven't grabbed his crotch in public to show him how it feels.

I haven't stood up indignantly and marched myself out of there.

When considering which one thing on the list above she could try, Carla made some lighthearted jokes about the trouble with armored clothing these days. Then, more seriously, she decided that wherever she was the next time John grabbed at her in public, she would be willing to get up and leave.

"That's great," we said. Then we encouraged her to turn her idea into a full-blown answer by relying on the coaching cues in chapter 2. We also recommended that she put any distracting thoughts or worries that cropped up into the right hand margin. Carla developed her answer to Question 5 as follows:

Question 5:	Answer:	Distracting Thoughts and Worries:
How can I actually get that?		No matter how I say this, I'm afraid it's
• When, where, under what circumstances?	Sunday, on our way home from church, I could start by	going to sound like I'm trying to get even
• Specify your actions.	telling John that I love him	with him. I don't want
• Brainstorm if you're stuck.	very much but that I can't take being grabbed or goosed in public any more. Then I could say something like, "I want you to know what I am going to do if it happens again." And to keep myself from worrying that he'll think my plan is just a way to get back at him— which it isn't—I'll go ahead	this to sound like a "because you were mean to me, I'm going to be even meaner to you" thing. I hope **saying** I'm going to do this is enough to get him to stop. It'll be hard to follow through but I
• Keep your goal in mind.	and say, "John, my goal here is	will because doing
• Rehearse blame-free statement.	to get you to stop grabbing at me in public, **not** to get even	nothing is worse.
• Handle worries.	with you. Then I'll explain that	
• Rehearse again.	the next time it happens I'd say, "I don't feel well and need to go home," after which I'd leave. And I'll also tell John that if it happens a second time, I'll go further and tell the people we were with that "I'm so embarrassed I need to go home now." Then I'll get up and leave.	But what if I do all this and he **still** grabs at me?

When she finished writing, Carla turned her attention to the last question:

Question 6: And if that doesn't work, what else can I do?

If my first plan doesn't work and John continues to grab at me, I could build on what I've already done and tell him that the next time he grabs at me, I'll announce to our friends that he and I feel differently about how to touch one another in public and that since I haven't been able to get through to him, whenever it happens, I just leave.

Outcome

"I wish I could say it only took one time for John to realize I meant business. And I wish I could tell you that this whole thing went smoothly. But it took a lot longer than I thought it might before John stopped his grabbing behavior. Also, it was more difficult for me to say those things out loud in front of other people than I even imagined it would be. I'm a private person and speaking out like that about our problem was so hard that I stuttered and felt myself trembling. But I did it. And I'm glad I did.

"Besides the fact that John no longer grabs at me in public, standing up for myself was good in another way. It gave me some of my pride and dignity back. I didn't notice how much I needed that or how important it is to feel good about yourself. But now I try to keep that in mind whenever I'm deciding whether I can put up with something or not.

"I actually had to speak up three times and use my back-up plan before John finally stopped. Part of the reason it took so long was because the first time that I said I didn't feel well and walked out the door, I got all the way to the car before I realized I didn't have the keys. It was too cold to stand around outside so I had to go back in and ask John to take me home. He sort of snickered to himself and made me wait another ten minutes before we left. (After that, when we went out, I put the spare keys in my purse.)

"At that point, I almost folded. But one of the coaching cues—'Keep your goal in mind,'—stuck with me and sort of propped me back up so I could see this thing all the way through.

"Now, of course, I'm glad that I kept going. I think what helped as much as what I said and did was what happened after I left. The other people who were there started telling John that it isn't okay to do that even in fun to a woman. I'm not sure, but I think that's what finally got through to him. All I care about is that he doesn't do that grabbing stuff at all now.

"I never did tell John that his goosing me was such a turn off that I had started shutting down sexually toward him. That was probably a good thing since it's not a problem any more."

Observations

Carla's decision to change the way she reacted to John's actions (rather than continue trying to convince him to change) was central to her ability to break the stalemate. Here is what also contributed to her success: before she put her plan into motion, Carla explained to John what she was going to do differently in the future and why. And then she left the choice about how things would play out up to him. It seems to us that by making the connection between *what* she was going to do and *why* she was going to do it crystal clear, Carla was able to prevent misunderstandings, keep the doors of communication open, and reduce the likelihood that things would escalate into a tit-for-tat cycle.

The Internet Effect

When Colin, a man in his late thirties, sat down at his home computer one evening, he was so intent on looking up the latest football scores that he forgot to change the user name and inadvertently logged on using his wife's screen name. Suddenly, he was besieged with sexually explicit instant messages from men he'd never heard of who thought they were chatting with his wife, Donna.

"What got me wasn't just that these men were writing things like that to my wife. Though that was bad enough, what hurt more was realizing Donna had been getting this kind of attention from strange men for God knows how long!

"When I confronted her, she said that what she was doing isn't any different than me looking at a men's magazine centerfold. Then she said that how she spends her time on the computer is her personal business and to leave her alone about it.

"'No way,' I said. 'You have no idea how it feels to be on the receiving end of this!' But she refused to discuss it. And since then, I've been confused and miserable. I rarely sleep through the night. Maybe once a week, I hear Donna go online for hours before she comes to bed, and it drives me crazy.

"You'd think our sex life would have suffered. But it's fine—actually, better than fine. And our everyday life seems as normal to me as it always has. However, my thoughts about our marriage are different now. Whenever we're intimate, I find myself wondering what's going on in her mind and I feel worried.

"I don't know what to do. Donna says there is no reason for us to go to a marriage counselor. She insists everything is fine—that I have nothing to worry about. And she acts just the same as always around me. But her forays into cyberspace feel ominous to me—it's like something in our marriage feels broken.

"I admit I read men's magazines sometimes. So what? It's not the same as talking to real people, for crying out loud. The pictures are fantasy. I turn to my wife for the real thing.

"I came to this workshop because I want to figure out some way to get my wife to stop talking to strange men on the Internet."

Below are Colin's written answers to the six questions. The coaching cues he found helpful are noted in parenthesis.

Question 1: What are my negative feelings?

Shocked. Confused. Can't eat. Can't sleep. (*Toward whom?*) *Angry* at her because she won't talk about this. *Wondering* if she thinks something's wrong with our marriage. *Worried* she wants something in the sex department she doesn't think she's getting from me.

Question 2: What's the fairest way to describe the problem?

(*We are different.*) We are different when it comes to how we feel about Internet sex talk. I say that it is wrong. Donna says it is as harmless as me reading men's magazines. I want her to stop doing it. She will not agree to that.

Question 3: Why do I want to work things out?

So I can trust my wife, (*Focus on positive feelings and/or practical reasons.*) ~~stop wondering what she's doing online,~~ get my marriage back on track, and start eating and sleeping like a normal person again.

Question 4: How would I like things between us to be?

I'd like us to ~~get out of crisis mode and~~ *(Turn what you* don't *want into what you* do *want.)* do what we can to repair this marriage. I would like to be in a marriage where ~~my wife doesn't get turned on by other men before she comes to bed with me. And I would like our marriage to be the kind where~~ whatever we do that is sexually stimulating is something we do together, ~~not separately~~. *(Specify your partner's realistic actions.)* I'd like Donna to watch X-rated movies with me ~~instead of going upstairs to chat with people on the Internet.~~ And I'd like her to say I'm the only man she needs.

Question 5: How can I actually get that?

First, get rid of the computer. *(Keep your goal in mind.)* I know that won't solve the problem, but it would give me some short-term relief. Then, maybe I could get her to be so happy with just me that she'd be fine giving up her Internet chats. *(Specify your actions.)* I could stop at a video store and rent some X-rated movies. But I'd need to get her in the mood first. Back in the old days, Donna liked it when I showed up with fresh-cut flowers and took her out for romantic dinners. So I could wine and dine her for a few nights. I know the way to get her in the mood is talk first, and then the X-rated movies and sex.

Question 6: And if that doesn't work, what else can I do?

Insist on her coming to see a marriage counselor or a couple's sex therapist with me. I'll do that if nothing else works.

Outcome

"At first, my plan seemed to be working fine. I made reservations for us for three nights in a row at really sensational restaurants. The first night we went out we had wine, laughed a little, ate great food, and went home feeling happy with each other. The second night went pretty much the same way, except that I had a dozen white roses delivered to her before I got home from work that day and we went dancing after dinner. I thought my plan was going great. But the third night we went out, I could tell something was wrong as soon as we got to the restaurant.

"Donna hardly spoke during dinner. And she hardly ate. Finally, she said she wanted to go home. I asked if anything was wrong, and she threw her napkin down on the table and said angrily, 'Why are you suddenly taking me out all the time? I want to know now! Are you having an affair? Are you dying of some terminal disease? Are you being transferred to a third-world nation? What? What's going on here? What's wrong?'

"'Nothing's wrong,' I told her. 'I just wanted to prove to you that I can make you happy. I want you to see that you don't need anyone else to make you feel special.'

"'I already know that, so now tell me what's *really* going on here?' she demanded.

"'Well obviously you *don't* know that,' I exploded, 'or you'd give up that Internet-sex-chat stuff that you do.'

"'So that's what's behind all these expensive dinners?' she said. 'You're pathetic! Take me home *now!*'

"I felt as if my idea of wining and dining her had been a catastrophic mistake. I was kicking myself for having failed to figure out another way to win her back. Things seemed even worse when we got home because Donna started up again.

"'I can't believe you even have the nerve to say you want me to stop going into online chat rooms when *you* watch dirty movies and read girlie magazines without any complaints from me!' she said.

"'That's just something I do to heighten the mood sometimes. Besides,' I countered, 'you're in the room when I do that! I'm not off in another room talking to other people.'

"'You want to be included?' she said. 'Stay in the room when I go online—there's no law that says you have to leave!'

"When she first said that, I thought the idea was crazy. But curiosity got to me and late one night a week later, when I heard Donna sit down at the computer, I went into the den and watched her chat. It was different than I thought it would be. She signs into a chat room where everyone pretends to be someone else, and they say these outrageous things just to make each other laugh or blush. When I found myself laughing out loud at one point, Donna turned to me and asked what I thought she should type in response. For a while we joined forces thinking of things to say in that chat room. It was a turn-on for both of us.

"Now that I understand what a chat room's like, I'm not worried that my marriage is doomed. The problem got settled when Donna said I could be in the same room when she goes online.

"Obviously, back when I was answering the six questions, joining her in her chatroom activity isn't how I planned to straighten things out. But deciding to wine and dine Donna like in the old days wasn't such a total loss. At least it got me to stop moping around the house, wishing the problem would go away but not doing anything about it."

Observations

Colin's story illustrates that even when the effort that goes into answering the six questions leads to a less-than-ideal plan, putting a plan into motion can jiggle the doors of communication open and set the relationship moving in an unanticipated new direction. However, things might not have worked out so well if Colin hadn't done one thing in particular: tell his wife the truth when she demanded to know, "What's going on here?" When Colin responded honestly saying, "I want you to see that you don't need anyone else to make you feel special," and "obviously you don't know that or you'd give up that Internet-sex-chat stuff that you do," he made it possible for the two of them to begin addressing the issues that divided them.

If he'd been unwilling to tell the truth in that moment, Colin might well have said something like, "I don't know what you mean. There's nothing going on." And if he had done that, we think his problem might still be keeping him up at night.

Putting Up with Public Put Downs

Jeanette, a woman in her late sixties, had been married to Aaron for almost fifty years when she signed up for our workshop and shared this story with us:

"My children are grown and married with families of their own. Aaron and I used to be history professors. We're retired now. When we're alone, my husband is quite nice to me. We discuss the news of the day, places we'd like to visit, what we think of the Rabbi's latest sermon, things like that. And he often asks my opinion. But when others are around, he's a different man. He's rude and sarcastic to me, and he puts down any idea I come up with.

"Obviously, I am not about to leave the old goat over this or I'd have done so by now. I love Aaron. But still, I would like to see if I can get him to be nicer to me in public."

Watching Jeanette answer the basic questions and come up with wonderfully innovative ideas about how to solve her problem delighted us. See if you feel the same way:

Question 1: What are my negative feelings?
Sick and tired of being discounted by my husband when others are around. *Mad* enough about it to come to this workshop!

Question 2: What's the fairest way to describe the problem?
(*We are different.*) We're different when it comes to how we acknowledge each other. I thank my husband when he makes suggestions or shares his ideas whether people are around or not. Aaron thanks *me* only if we are alone. I want him to start thanking me even when other people are around. I've mentioned this to him before, but he just tunes me out. I don't like being tuned out, and that is another part of this problem.

Question 3: Why do I want to work things out?
~~I'd hate to think that the first time anyone will hear my husband compliment me will be when he's reading my eulogy~~! (*Focus on positive feelings and/or practical reasons.*) It'd be nice to hear Aaron say he likes some of my ideas in front of other people. That would make me smile and feel appreciated in ways that are different from how I feel when he thanks me in private.

Question 4: How would I like things between us to be?
~~Instead of him waving me off or greeting what I say with sarcastic remarks,~~ (*Turn what you* don't *want into what you* do *want.*) I'd like both of us to make overt, positive acknowledgments of each other's comments, thoughts, and opinions. (*Specify your partner's realistic actions.*) I'd like Aaron to give me

credit in public for the ideas I bring up. I'd like him to say things like, "That's a good idea, Jeanette," or, "Thanks, glad you thought of that." And I'd like him to apologize if he delivers one of his sarcastic put downs.

Question 5: How can I actually get that?

(*When, where, under what circumstances?*) I imagine I could wait until the next time we're out with people we know really well, like our friends Kate and Joe. We have brunch with them at least twice a week. Then, (*Specify your actions.*) I'd interrupt my husband the moment he waves me off and say, "Aaron, your opinion matters to me. In fact, what you say matters a great deal to me. That's why I'd like to hear you give me credit in public for the ideas I bring up. I'd like to hear you say things like, "That's a good idea, Jeanette," or, "Thanks, glad you thought of that."

And if Aaron doesn't do that, I'd interrupt again and say, "Dear, I want you to read this aloud." Then I'd hand him one of the cards I'd prepared in advance where I'd written out good responses for him to say. I'd pick the one I'd like him to say at that moment.

Question 6: And if that doesn't work, what else can I do?

Even if I wait 'til we're with Kate and Joe, this plan might embarrass him terribly, which is neither my intention nor my wish. But if it happens, I'll say I'm sorry, but that I will continue doing this until he acknowledges me and my ideas in a positive way when others are around.

Outcome

About a month after the workshop, Jeanette sent us this handwritten note:

"My dears, this plan worked like a charm, first time out! Poor old guy was so shocked when I interrupted him (not something that happens often to a professor unless you raise your hand first) that his jaw dropped. But to his credit, when Aaron saw that I was serious, he apologized and thanked me for my comments. I didn't even need the index cards I'd made.

"Since things got straightened out so easily, I guess you're wondering why I waited so long to resolve this with Aaron. That's easy to explain. Maybe the answer to my problem *was* inside me all the time, but before an answer can come out, you have to ask the right question. Thanks for giving me six 'right' questions to ask."

Observations

Even if you come up with a terrific plan, getting to a positive outcome requires that you act from a position of goodwill and that you express your genuine, positive feelings and intentions directly to the other person. That's exactly what Jeanette did so effectively in this story. We especially liked the way she combined her positive feelings for Aaron with her request that he change his behavior— "Aaron, your opinion matters to me—in fact, what you say matters a great deal to me. That's why I'd like you to give me credit in public for the ideas I bring up."

We believe that when you are trying to improve some aspect of your relationship, the more fully you express your positive intentions, the more likely it is that your partner will consider your words, hear your concerns, and be open to participating in a solution.

Grave Troubles

Although she seemed to be paying attention, Maryanne, a tall woman who appeared to be in her forties, kept her thoughts to herself during much of the workshop. It was several months later when we received a long letter from her that we learned how our presentation had affected her. Here are Maryanne's words:

"When you started off your workshop saying that you enjoy hearing from people who apply your suggestions to their relationship problems, I had no intention of being one of those people! At first, I wasn't sure why I even came to your workshop. When I signed up, all I remember thinking was that the topic sounded interesting.

"My husband, Bill, and I had one of those marriages that go along on its own. I wasn't able to talk to him about anything really important but, unlike everyone else who showed up for your workshop, I didn't have a specific problem in mind that needed solving.

"I think I only half-listened to what you were saying about the first three questions. But when you got to Question 4 (*How would I like things between us to be?*) I was hooked.

"The background to all this is something that happened six months before your workshop. Bill was away on a ski trip in Colorado with some of his men friends and I was up north in Maine visiting my family. My mother was quite ill at the time and, sadly, a few days after I arrived, she died. I called Bill and told him what happened and said that I wanted him to come to Maine and be there with me for the funeral, which was going to be the next day. He said he'd check with the airlines and call me back.

"An hour later he phoned and said he couldn't get a flight out that would get him there on time for the funeral, so there was no sense in coming to Maine and he'd just see me at home the next week.

"I think the shock of losing my mother robbed me of the strength to protest. But I was aware that I was terribly disappointed, although not surprised. I'd always let him wiggle out of family events. For years, I'd tried to convince myself not to get angry about this and to accept that he was raised very differently and that he didn't have the same sense of family that I did. He didn't even go to his own family's events. That's just the way he was.

"Bill got home from his ski trip the day after I got back from Maine. When he tried to offer his condolences, I let him have it. I gave him an earful about having to go through my mother's funeral and all the decision making that came next by myself while he was off gallivanting out west with his buddies.

"After that, Bill went out of his way not to do or say anything that might set me off. Eventually I calmed down and went back to behaving as I'd always had. But the anger I felt toward Bill was still there. I was irritable and a lot less loving.

And every once in a while, when I was packing to go to an anniversary dinner or a milestone birthday celebration for one of my relatives up north, I'd realize I really was tired of going to these events without my husband. I was sick of making excuses for him to myself and to my other family members. I was tired of being the only relative who always showed up alone.

"So when you were talking about how to answer, 'How would I like things between us to be?' I flashed on my mother's funeral and remembered standing there at her open grave all alone, the only one who didn't have someone's arm around her to comfort her. Then I flashed forward to the day that my father will be buried and I thought, *I don't ever want to be standing at a gravesite all by myself again without someone to put his arm around me.*

"I realized how much I wanted my husband to come to family functions with me. I wanted him to be there at all the happy *and* all the sad events. And suddenly, I knew how I'd like things to be and why I had come to your workshop.

"I didn't do things exactly like you talked about in your workshop. In fact, I only wrote out my answers to the last two questions. And I answered them out of order. Before I could write out an answer to Question 5, I felt that I needed to answer Question 6. I needed to consider what I'd do if Bill refused to start joining me at my family functions."

"Here's what I wrote when I got home:"

Question 6: And if that doesn't work, what else can I do?

If Bill won't come to Maine with me, why stay married? I'll divorce him and get a new husband. I really will. I'm not going to grow older feeling more and more alone with Bill when other husbands (like my two sisters') are happy to be part of their wife's family.

Question 5: How can I actually get that?

I can start a discussion with Bill at dinner, where he's a captive audience, and say, "Remember those vows we took about 'in sickness and in health'? Well, we've arrived at one version of the sickness and health thing. My family is getting older and sicker and I need you to be there for me." (I'm not going to say, "Shape up or ship out. Knowing I'd move on without him rather than live with things as they are gives me a lot of comfort, but it doesn't need to be said aloud.)

Then I'd say, "Bill, in the past I have tried to guilt you into coming with me or argue you into it or pretend it doesn't matter to me. But that hasn't worked. So now, because I believe that when you appeal to a person's higher nature, they come through, I'm going to ask you to be the wonderful husband I think you are and to start coming with me to my family's events from now on and to be polite while you're there."

"I thought my answer to Question 5 was pretty good and that it would get me what I wanted without a struggle. But I was wrong. After I said all those things, Bill said, 'What do you want from me? I can't undo what's been done! I didn't come to your mother's funeral. It's over. Nothing I can do now is going to fix that, so stop being angry at me and let's just go back to how things were before all of this started.'

"I dug in my heels and said, 'You don't want to pay a price for me being angry about all the times before when you've said "no". And I don't want to pay a price in the future by being alone at family gatherings! You're my family as much as they are and I want you there with me. I don't want to pretend that this is all right. It's not.'

"'So instead you want me to pretend that I'm happy to do this for you?' he asked.

"'Yes. That's exactly what I want,' I told him. 'And I don't want you to use this as a you-owe-me bargaining chip against me. I've been pretending to be okay with your choice not to come with me for decades. Now it's your turn. You pretend your way through this for the next thirty years—and then we'll talk about it again.'

"Right then Bill's eyes grew wide as if the truth about how unhappy I'd been about this for all these years hit him for the first time. He took a deep breath and said, 'Okay.'

"So Bill has agreed to come with me to visit my family at holidays and celebrations and to be there in bad times to come. He's not going to gripe or complain about it—he promised. All I had to promise in return was to stop thanking him. He said it was really starting to annoy him...but he put his arm around me when he said that."

Observations

We believe that asking and answering all six questions in the order in which they are presented to you here is a great way to access your best thoughts about how to solve your problem. However, Maryanne's experience suggests that even if you skip or half-heartedly answer the first three questions, thinking about your answer to Question 4 (*How would I like things between us to be?*) can point you in the right direction. In this story, thinking about how she'd like things to be helped Maryanne recognize that she wanted more out of her marriage. And then she set out to get that.

This story makes another important point. If, after you've answered Question 4 (*How would I like things between us to be?*), your belief that your partner will not step in to help settle things is keeping you stuck, it may help to answer Question 6 *(And if that doesn't work, what else can I do?)* before you answer Question 5 *(How can I actually get that?)*. When Maryanne changed the order of the last two questions, she was prompted to develop an if-all-else-fails-back-up plan, assuring herself that she could handle the problem on her own if necessary. Knowing that relaxed her enough to move on and answer Question 5.

THOUGHTS TO TAKE WITH YOU

When your partner's behavior is unacceptable, an effective approach calls for you to:

- Alter the way in which you react to the objectionable behavior.
- Choose the high road and operate from a place of goodwill.
- Tell your partner—in advance—what you are going to do differently.
- Avoid sugar-coating, side-stepping, or blaming statements.
- Work to unearth your subtle feelings (Question 1).

7

Sex: Too Much, Too Little, Too Inept, Too Weird

Altering and improving your lovemaking experience

When it comes to talking with our partners about the most intimate aspect of our relationship—sex—many of us don't know how or where to begin. And that's too bad because mutually satisfying lovemaking seldom "just happens." At a minimum, it requires that we establish reciprocal trust and that we have the desire to please. Even when it's fireworks and home runs in the beginning, maintaining truly joyful and fulfilling sexual relations calls for partners to talk to one another about their wants, needs, likes, and dislikes. This is a chapter about how to do that—truthfully, effectively, and without fear of wounding the other person.

While the stories you will find here present issues that were resolved cooperatively by both partners, asking and answering the basic questions can help you begin to settle your sexual differences even when the other person is reluctant to discuss the problem. To understand this point, you need only reread "Adored but Bored," in chapter 3.

Below you will find stories from four of the people we met when we spoke at a daylong seminar about intimacy. All of these men and women were in respectful, largely positive relationships. And all of them wanted mutually satisfying sexual relations with their partner. Their accounts present both sides of the same conflict. One of these deals with a couple's different levels of sexual desire. The other examines the toll that traumatic childhood experiences have had on one partner's ability to enjoy sex.

We hope that reading their experiences encourages you to ask and answer the basic questions. Over and over again, we have found that when people do this, their answers point them toward direct, relaxed, and effective ways to initiate a discussion about even the most sensitive of sexual difficulties.

Was It as Good for You?

Monica and Wayne are a thirty-something couple who have been married for fifteen years. They came to this seminar at Wayne's insistence. What follows is a condensed version of their separate views of their problem. Monica explains:

"I have a wonderful, but *very* horny husband. Sex has always been a top priority for him. It used to be for me, too. But lately, my sex drive has been decreasing. It isn't that I don't like sex; it's just that I'm too stressed out to enjoy it like I used to. I stay pretty tense during the work week. My sex drive only improves when I've got a long weekend or when we're on vacation.

"These days, what I want more than sex is some old-fashioned, nonsexual physical affection. I wish I could be more affectionate with Wayne, but he's always so horny that I'm afraid to hug him or even brush up against him in case he thinks that it's an invitation to have sex. I only put my head on his shoulder when we are in situations where it's not possible to be sexual. Otherwise, I keep my distance—especially when it gets close to bedtime. And if that doesn't discourage him, sometimes I'll say 'no,' which makes me feel guilty. There are other times when I'll say 'yes,' but my heart's not in it and I'm afraid it shows. Wayne says he's not angry that I'm not interested in sex as often as I used to be, but he sure acts like he is."

Wayne describes the problem this way:

"I married a beautiful, sexy woman. I was thrilled that she enjoyed sex as much as I do. So when Monica started getting a lot less interested in sex, I was confused. She says she's too stressed out during the week, and I don't get that at all. Seems to me, having sex is how you reduce anxiety and stress.

"There are some nights when I practically have to beg Monica for sex. And I resent that! She thinks I shouldn't take it so personally when she says 'no.' But as far as I'm concerned, it *is* personal. What could be *more* personal than sex?"

When they'd finished giving us their respective views of the problem, we talked about the importance of noticing and moving beyond the grip of the negative emotions that are attached to our disputes with one another. Then, we asked Monica and Wayne separately to list the negative feelings they had about their dilemma (they did not share their lists with one another), and here is what they wrote:

Question 1: What are my negative feelings?

Monica's Answer:	Wayne's Answer:
Annoyed when he pressures me. **Guilty** when I say 'no.' Worse when I say 'yes' because I find myself just waiting for it to be over and that leaves me **ashamed**.	**Pissed** that I have to practically beg for sex. **Worried** that I don't turn her on anymore. **Wondering** if there's something physically or mentally wrong with her.

Next, we gave Monica and Wayne copies of Questions 2 and 3 and asked them to write out their personal answers to those questions. We also gave each of them a separate piece of paper to jot down any distracting thoughts or feelings that popped up along the way. To make this a safe and honest experience, we instructed them to keep their lists of distractions to themselves.

Below you will find their individual written responses to Questions 2 and 3 along with their separately created lists of distractions. The coaching cues we gave them are noted in parentheses.

Question 2: What's the fairest way to describe the problem?

Monica's Answer:	Monica's Distracting Thoughts and Worries:
(We are different.) We are different in terms of what we want from each other—especially during the week. Wayne wants to have sex, and I just want to cuddle. He tries to convince me to have sex when I don't feel like it, which makes me tense and unhappy.	I'm tired of Wayne making it so difficult for me to say 'no.' Once in a while, I actually fake having an orgasm just so his feelings won't be hurt. And I hate faking orgasms.

Wayne's Answer:	Wayne's Distracting Thoughts and Worries:
(We are different.) We're different in our sex drives. I want sex more often than she does. Lately, I never know how she's going to react when I make my move and it's stressing me out.	There has to be something wrong for her to become so disinterested in sex and so removed from me all the time.

Question 3: Why do I want to work things out?

Monica's Answer:	Monica's Distracting Thoughts and Worries:
~~So Wayne will stop pressuring me for sex when I'm not in the mood.~~ (Focus on positive feelings and/or practical reasons.) It would be so nice just to hug and be affectionate with him some nights.	I may not be interested in sex on work nights—but I miss hugging and kissing.

Wayne's Answer:	Wayne's Distracting Thoughts and Worries:
(Focus on positive feelings and/or practical reasons.) I want our sex life to be like it used to be.	I don't want to seem like some sex-crazed maniac—but the less Monica wants sex, the more I want it.

Before Monica and Wayne began to write out their separate answers to Question 4, we let them know that when they finished, we would be asking them to share their written responses to this question with one another. We went on to explain that they would build on what they'd written individually to create a joint answer to the question. We also reminded them to continue to privately jot down any interfering, unkind, or irrelevant concerns that came to mind.

Their separate answers follow:

Question 4: How would I like things between us to be?

Monica's Answer:	Monica's Distracting Thoughts and Worries:
I'd like us to be more relaxed and more affectionate during the week. **(Specify your partner's realistic actions.)** I'd like Wayne to put his arm around me while we watch TV and hug me when he gets home from work. And if I'm not in the mood for sex, I'd like him to kiss me and say, "Okay honey, I love you. Get some sleep now."	I can't even put my head on his shoulder and cuddle with him any more. The minute we touch, Wayne's ready to go at it. Why can't I have more affection without having to have sex?

Wayne's Answer:	Wayne's Distracting Thoughts and Worries:
When I'm stressed out, **(Specify your partner's realistic actions.)** I'd like Monica to consider having a "quickie" even if she isn't up for a whole night of sex.	I'm all for mutual pleasuring, but if she's not interested when I am, why not have a quickie? What's wrong with that?

After reading each other's answers, Monica and Wayne told us that seeing what each had written down like that crystallized what they already knew—they were at odds about how often to have sex. But it also showed them something they hadn't known—they both wanted to reduce stress and feel more relaxed.

At that point they moved on to jointly develop the answer below:

Question 4: How would I (we) like things between us to be?

"We'd like to feel less stress during the week and we'd like to be more balanced in our desire for sex and physical affection. (*What would the perfect partner do?*) 'Perfect partners' would be sensitive to each other's moods and needs and they would ask each other questions. For example, the husband would ask, 'How sexual are you feeling tonight?' If the wife says she isn't feeling sexual, the husband would ask, 'Is there anything I could do to get you more in the mood?'

If the wife says 'no' he would accept that without a fuss. He would smile and say, 'Okay then.'

"In another example, the wife would ask, 'Could you cuddle up with me now without feeling like you have to have sex tonight?' If the husband says 'no,' the wife would accept this without a fuss. She would smile and say, "Okay then.""

Noticing that neither Monica nor Wayne had distracting thoughts or feelings as they worked on their response, we asked if they would be willing to answer the two remaining questions together. They agreed to try, and here's what they wrote:

Question 5: How can I (we) actually get that?

Every evening, before we even have a chance to worry about what's going to happen or not happen that night—(*When, where, and under what circumstances?*) while we are still at the dinner table—we can ask each other what we'd like in terms of sex or cuddling that night. (*Specify your actions.*) Then, on nights when we find out that we don't want the same things, we can try to do the following:

1) We can decide to do nothing, and without pressuring each other, be pleasant about it and just keep checking with each other each evening until we both want the same things.

Or else this is what we can try:

2) Wayne can, as a gift to Monica, cuddle with her and not have sex.

3) Monica can, as a gift to Wayne, have a quickie.

Monica's Distracting Thoughts and Worries:	Wayne's Distracting Thoughts and Worries:
But if I say "no" to having sex more often than he'd like, what's to keep Wayne from getting angry and arguing with me?	Cuddling is fine, but what if it makes me horny?

Question 6: And if that doesn't work, what else can I (we) do?

Wayne can take care of his needs on his own in the bathroom, and Monica can give herself a hug. (*Handle worries.*) And later on, to keep the things light and relaxed, one of us can ask the other, "Was it as good for you as it was for me?"

Monica's Distracting Thoughts and Worries:	Wayne's Distracting Thoughts and Worries:
I'm not sure this will work. But I hope it does.	This is not ideal—just better than how things stand now.

Outcome

While we don't know what happened for Monica and Wayne after the seminar, we do remember seeing them smile as they left. And when we read their work-shop evaluation form, so did we. Next to the question, "How would you rate this portion of the seminar?" they'd written, *Hope it was as good for you as it was for us. Thanks!*

Observations

We believe that when partners of goodwill bring their answers together as they try to work things out, they often begin to think about and talk about their problems differently. And they do so without making one person wrong and the other one right. As we already have said, people who are approached in a blame-free manner are more likely to feel motivated to find ways to resolve things. Some of Monica's comments on her workshop evaluation form bear this out:

"Looking at Wayne's answer to Question 4 (*How would I like things between us to be?*) made me think about things in a different light. Seeing that piece of paper with his handwriting scrawled all over as he wrote out exactly how he'd like things to be tugged at my heart. Reading about how he felt was more pow-erful than hearing him say it. It got to me so much that instead of wanting to get this problem taken care of so I'd be more relaxed, I wanted to get it taken care of so both of us would feel better."

Wayne also wrote about reading his wife's answer to Question 4. "That's when, instead of this being about how much sex to have, it turned into how to reduce the stress we both felt and how to give each other more of what we had said we'd like."

No Sex for the Foreseeable Future

Lori and Jason, the parents of two girls under the age of ten, have been married for twelve years. They told us that showing up for this seminar was a big step for them. Quietly, Lori explained:

"From the time I was very young until I was in my late teens, my father molested me. I never told anyone back then. And as soon as I was old enough, I moved out of my father's house. My plan was never again to think about what happened. I put it behind me and moved on.

"I never told a soul, not even Jason, until seven months ago. I still might not have told him except that suddenly it seemed as if every time the television came on, there was another story about child abuse or incest. Between the talk shows, the news, and some of those prime-time series, I started coming apart at the seams. A story would come on and either I'd find myself unable to tear my eyes away from the TV or I would grab for the remote and start channel surfing like mad. I tried to act like everything was fine, but I couldn't pull it off.

"Maybe because all those television reports were so graphic or maybe because our daughters were the age that I'd been when things were so awful for me or—or who knows why...all I knew was that I was losing my grip. Every night after I put the girls to sleep, all I did was sit in a chair and hug myself. I barely spoke, and I refused to go out of the house except for carpooling the kids.

"Jason was getting really worried about me, and still I wouldn't tell him what was on my mind. I was afraid he'd be disgusted by me. And I thought he'd go after my father, and then the kids would lose their grandfather. At the very least, I knew Jason would refuse to go to any more family gatherings, and then I'd have to explain things to my children, my siblings, my mother—it was too much. I tried to just put it all out of my mind. But the harder I tried, the worse things got.

"Before this, I never really enjoyed sex all that much, but at least I could fake my way through it. All of a sudden, I found that I couldn't do that, so I started avoiding sex. I'd pick a fight with Jason as soon as he got home from work so he wouldn't want to come near me. Or else I'd sit and babble to him about things I knew he found boring. Or I'd fake being sick and contagious. But after a while, we were so distant from each other and I was acting so strangely all the time that Jason said either I tell him what was going on or I get myself into therapy. I'd always told people therapy was not for me. I said it was for those who had more money and fewer friends than I. But the truth is, I was afraid of what might happen if I opened up old wounds. When Jason gave me an ultimatum, I was more afraid of telling him what was going on in me than of going into therapy, so I got the name of a psychologist and made an appointment.

"The therapist was a good listener. She helped me get up the nerve to tell Jason the truth, and she sat right there with me when I told him. She also helped me find the courage to say something that no wife should ever have to say to her husband—because it isn't fair. I told him that I didn't want to have sex and I didn't know how long I would feel that way and that I didn't want him to have an affair in the meantime."

Lori's eyes filled with tears then and she seemed too choked up to continue, so Jason jumped in and added his thoughts to hers:

"Back when Lori started acting so strangely, I had no idea what was going on. Some days I was concerned about her. Other days I was just angry because she was shutting me out and I didn't know why or what to do. I hated saying, 'Go to a therapist or we're through,' but I was desperate to get her to start dealing with things. We couldn't go on like that. Even the girls could tell something was wrong, and I didn't know how to answer their questions.

"The day that Lori asked me to come with her to see her therapist I was really afraid she was going to tell me she had found someone else. Why else would she stay so far away from me and never want to have sex? Then, when she hid her face and told me what that son-of-a-bitch had done to her, I was so filled with love for her and rage at the people who had allowed this to happen that I held her close and we cried together.

"I told Lori she could take as long as she needed to heal from the past and that I would stay by her side. And I meant that. But another part of me was thinking, 'What am I supposed to do? I love her. I did say 'for better or worse,' and I take that seriously, but how long am I going to have to go without sex?'"

Lori touched Jason's hand briefly and said, "We've made a lot of progress since then, and I'm starting to feel safer. But we don't know how to start adding sex back into our marriage without putting pressure on me—so my therapist suggested we come to this seminar and just gather information. We were both surprised that there are other couples here with similar problems. But the thing is, we didn't know that a part of this seminar was about working on ways to solve things. I don't want to pressure myself by coming up with a plan I might not be able to follow. So we're just going to go through the motions, if that's okay."

We told Lori and Jason that moving forward at their own speed was the perfect way to do this. We said we understood that problem solving around issues of sex and past abuse can be uncomfortable at first, and we emphasized that we encourage people to decide how best and how quickly to proceed.

Then we asked Lori and Jason to write out their separate answers to Questions 1 through 3. We explained that these answers are not meant to be shared. Below you will find Lori's responses to the first three questions, followed by Jason's. In the left margin are the coaching cues that each relied upon.

Questions:	Lori's Answers:	Distracting Thoughts and Worries:
1. What are my negative feelings? • Pay attention to all negative feelings.	**Anxious** even thinking about adding sex back into our marriage. **Afraid** to try it again because I feel so much safer without sex. **Worried** that continuing on this way is too frustrating for Jason. **Afraid** not to add sex back in case Jason gets tired of living this way.	I don't know if I'll ever be normal enough to be the kind of wife that Jason deserves.
2. What's the fairest way to describe the problem? • Remove phrases implying you're stuck.	Our problem is about how ~~or even if~~ to be sexual again.	

Questions:	Lori's Answers:	Distracting Thoughts and Worries:
3. Why do I want to work things out? • Focus on positive feelings and/or practical reasons.	I want to be free of the past. I want to get on with my life. I want to work this out so I am able to make love to Jason ~~without freezing up or sobbing in fear.~~	I don't want that alcoholic SOB father of mine to win! I don't want him to ruin something I'm supposed to be able to enjoy.

Questions:	Jason's Answers:	Distracting Thoughts and Worries:
1. What are my negative feelings? • Pay attention to all your negative feelings.	This has been going on so long I don't know how I feel. I go from being **concerned** and **understanding** to **irritated** and **impatient** for things to get better.	
2. What's the fairest way to describe the problem?	Lori and I don't have sex anymore, and I want to, but I can't figure out when or how to change that.	
3. Why do I want to work things out? • Focus on positive feelings and/or practical reasons.	I want to work this out so we can have a normal life.	Not sure we ever will.

At this point, we asked them to separately write out their answers to Question 4 and then share what they'd written with one another. We reminded them to continue privately jotting down any distracting thoughts or worries that showed up along the way. After that, Lori and Jason created one combined answer to Questions 4, 5, and 6.

Question 4: How would I like things between us to be?

Lori's Answer: I would like us to ease back into being able to make love again. **(Specify your partner's realistic actions.)** I'd like Jason to agree to start slowly and to let me be completely in charge of how far things go. And if I feel uneasy for any reason, I want him to stop the minute I say that.	**Lori's Distracting Thoughts and Worries:** I can't even **think** about sex—how will I ever get over this? I want to be on the giving end of things, not the receiving end, for a long time—maybe forever.

Jason's Answer: I want things to be like they're supposed to be. I would like us to be sexual again. **(Specify your partner's realistic actions.)** I'd like Lori to concentrate on me and to block out thoughts that disturb her so we can make love without her thinking about the past. She could start by trying some of the safe, nonsexual touching exercises we read about that help other couples like us start to get close again.	**Jason's Distracting Thoughts and Worries:** I'm not sure if she's ready to try this, but I'm ready to do just about anything.

After reading each other's answers, Lori and Jason fashioned this answer together:

Question 4: How would I (we) like things between us to be?

We would like to be able to do things that lead us back to having a normal sex life. (*Specify your partner's realistic actions.*) Lori would like Jason to agree that she would be in charge of any physical contact they have—this means she'd be the person who decides when to start and when to stop. And she would like Jason to agree that when she is ready for sexual touching, in the beginning, she would be the giver and he would be the receiver. Jason would like Lori to know that he agrees to all of this. And he'd like Lori to try the nonsexual touching exercises they've read about.

Like many other partners, while combining their separate answers to Question 4, neither Lori nor Jason had distracting thoughts or feelings.

Question 5: How can I (we) actually get that?

(*Keep your goal in mind.*) To do things that get us back to a normal sex life, we could try the nonsexual touching exercises we've both read about. (*When, where, under what circumstances?*) We could do this a few days before our next meeting with Lori's therapist. (*Handle worries.*) Lori wouldn't feel safe unless we picked a *completely* nonsexual exercise that we could do in a lighted room for a very short amount of time. (*Specify your joint actions.*) One afternoon, we could take turns giving each other a five-minute foot rub and see how that goes.

Lori's Distracting Thoughts and Worries:	Jason's Distracting Thoughts and Worries:
What if every time I try something, I look up and see my father touching me instead of Jason? The lights have to be on.	Lori hasn't wanted to talk about any of this before. Hope it lasts.

Question 6: And if that doesn't work, what else can I (we) do?

We could try a different exercise. (*When, where, under what circumstances?*) We'd talk to Lori's therapist about it first. Then we could try something else the day before our next meeting with her. (*Specify your joint actions.*) We could also try what we heard about from another couple here—group therapy for incest survivors and their partners.

Lori's Distracting Thoughts and Worries:	Jason's Distracting Thoughts and Worries:
I didn't know that there were therapy groups for couples like us. If we went and if we saw others dealing with the same kinds of problems, maybe I wouldn't feel so guilty about how long it's taking me to get my act together.	I think we had better ask Lori's therapist about the group-therapy idea before doing something like that.

Outcome

When they finished the questions, Lori told us, "Even though we were just going to go through the motions, we ended up with something I'm actually okay with trying. The funny thing is, we've known about those touching exercises all along. But whenever Jason wanted to discuss them, it made me so nervous I just couldn't.

"Writing about the exercises was a lot different than talking about them. It was just easier. It felt more like we were considering ideas that we could erase at any moment and not like I'd actually have to do any of them. That made me a lot less anxious. Then I started picturing what I'd need in order to try those exercises. You know, like keeping it to five minutes or less, having the room all lit up, and making sure we'd be seeing my therapist shortly afterward. Once those things were added in, I didn't feel as anxious. And I'm surprised, but now I can really see myself trying some of those exercises."

Jason smiled and said, "I wasn't sure what we'd get out of answering this. We've been stuck for such a long time, I was worried we'd never get beyond this point. But now I'm more hopeful."

Observations

When Lori said, "Writing…felt more like we were just considering ideas that we could erase at any moment and not like I'd actually have to do any of them," we noticed another benefit to writing your answers down. Unlike what may happen when you're not quite ready to talk but you try to do that anyway, writing down the answers to the six questions—while holding an eraser in your hand—

lets you know that you can take back your words. And knowing that can make it a lot easier to put them out there in the first place.

THOUGHTS TO TAKE WITH YOU

When you want to create a safe and mutually satisfying sexual relationship:

- Talk with your partner in a location where it is not possible to be sexual.
- Combine your answers with your partner's. This can help couples of goodwill stop blaming and start pulling together more quickly.
- Consider getting professional help when dealing with abuse issues.
- Get as much information as you can from experienced professionals, books, seminars, etc.

8

Ex-Communications

Interactions with an ex-spouse that
put pressure on your marriage

The newly married couple snuggle on the couch enjoying an after dinner glass of wine. They are very much in love and are just about to kiss when the phone rings. The husband picks up the receiver, covers the mouthpiece, and whispers, "It's my ex." The new wife chokes on the sip of wine she'd been savoring and storms out of the room.

This scene mirrors the experiences of many of the remarried people we met while working on this chapter. Their accounts support the notion that when one or both partners in a new relationship have an ex-spouse, the simplest things can get complicated. So how do people keep their balance when connections to the past interfere with a present-day love?

Here you will see how one woman and two men, who were at odds with their partners over how best to deal with an ex-spouse, uncover calm, clear, and heartwarming ways to communicate their concerns and then come up with ideas that put both partners on the same side of the issue. At the start, each of these people believed that calmly coexisting with a past love while holding fast to the present one was a worthy goal. And none of them expected to get it right in this lifetime.

What the New Wife Wants

Kim and Jerry married eighteen months ago. Both are in their mid-thirties. This is Kim's first marriage and Jerry's second. Kim told us that she wanted Jerry to spend less time on the phone with his "ex." As her story unfolds below, notice how Kim's willingness to thoroughly answer Question 1 (*What are my negative feelings?*) set the stage for a successful resolution of her problem.

"My husband and his ex-wife, Roberta, have known each other since nursery school. When Jerry ended things with her three years ago, they didn't have any kids, and he gave her everything she wanted, so they parted on good terms.

"The trouble is that ever since Jerry and I got married, Roberta phones my husband about any little thing that's on her mind. And Jerry seems fine with all her calls. He talks to her almost every night for up to an hour while I sit around twiddling my thumbs.

"Want to know what happens when I complain? Jerry has the *nerve* to tell me I ought to be more understanding. He claims that all Roberta wants is advice about things like what kind of car to buy and how to know if she's getting a good deal. Then Jerry goes through his whole 'poor Roberta' routine. ('Poor Roberta is all alone in this world—no family at all—poor, poor Roberta.') He says, 'So she calls to talk to me every day. Can't you cut her some slack? She doesn't have anyone else.'

"I don't care who or what she doesn't have. I don't like the fact that Jerry spends so much time on the phone with her every night. No wife wants to keep coming in second with her own husband."

Kim jumped right into answering the six questions. Below are her written answers and the coaching cues that helped her shape her responses:

Question 1:	Answer:	Distracting Thoughts and Worries:
What are my negative feelings? • Toward whom? • Get rid of negative labels. • Eliminate **should/ shouldn't**. • Pay attention to all your negative feelings. • Replace blaming words.	**Angry** at Jerry because he ~~is so spineless that he~~ won't set limits with her. ~~He should know better, so should she!~~ **Frustrated** I can't get through to him. **Suspicious** ~~about why he's choosing her over me~~ and ~~that makes me~~ **insecure**.	How many phone calls will it take to make him see Roberta is too emotionally dependent on him? Maybe Jerry likes her needing him. Is there something more going on?

Question 2:	Answers:	Distracting Thoughts and Worries:
What's the fairest way to describe the problem? • We are different. • No blaming, explaining, or guessing. • Remove phrases implying you're stuck.	We are different when it comes to whether or not to set limits on Roberta's nightly calls. She calls practically every night. Jerry takes her calls. I want him to cut her back to one night a week or to limit the amount of time he stays on the phone, but he doesn't ~~seem to like that idea~~. So we fight about it. ~~Jerry acts like he doesn't want to spend time with me as much as I want to spend time with him. And if that's the case, there's not much I can do about it~~.	

Question 3:	Answers:	Distracting Thoughts and Worries:
Why do I want to work things out? • Focus on positive feelings and/or practical reasons.	So we can have the kind of marriage we said we wanted back when we got engaged— the kind of marriage where both of us devote most of our time and energy to each other ~~and not to a relationship from the past~~.	Jerry should want to spend evenings with me without interruptions from his ex-wife. I keep my phone calls short so I can spend more time with him. He could do that, too, if he wanted.

Question 4:	Answer:	Distracting Thoughts and Worries:
How would I like things between us to be? • Turn what you **don't** want into what you **do** want. • Specify your partner's realistic actions.	~~I don't want my married life to be filled with every night interruptions from Roberta.~~ I'd like us to spend more quiet time together. I would like Jerry to understand how I feel when I see him choosing her over me, and I'd like him to reassure me that I'm the number-one woman in his life. Specifically, he could say, "I love you more than anyone in the world. I want you to feel special and secure." I'd also like him to show me he means that by setting aside a large block of time in the evenings that's just for us—when he won't allow interruptions.	This is not going to happen unless Jerry wants it to. If he doesn't, then what am I doing here? Doesn't he get that I don't feel like I'm as important to him as Roberta is? He must know that. Nobody's that thick! Maybe he just doesn't care.

Question 5:	Answer:	Distracting Thoughts and Worries:
How can I actually get that? • Keep your goal in mind.	In order for Jerry to understand how I feel, he'd have to read my answers to all six of these questions. Just joking! Only I really don't know what to do. We can't talk about Roberta without landing in an argument so fast that we never get to the part where I say how I feel.	There's no way I could show Jerry my cross-outs. And I'd never be able to look him in the eyes again if he saw what I wrote here in this column.

Question 5: (cont.)	Answer:	Distracting Thoughts and Worries:
• When, where, under what circumstances?	So maybe before I go home today, I could copy all my answers over (but leave out the crossed-out words and the things in the distractions margin). Then put them in an envelope. In the morning, I could give the envelope to Jerry and ask him not to read it until he gets to his office. That way, he would be able to know what I'm feeling without us having a fight. But I'd have to phrase things carefully and gently so he'd read my answers all the way through. I think I could do that.	What if he reads it and gets mad or ends up thinking less of me?
• Specify your actions.		
• Handle worries.		What if he reads it and nothing changes at all?
• Rehearse blame-free statement.		

Question 6:	Answer:	Distracting Thoughts and Worries:
And if that doesn't work, what else can I do?	If Jerry reads all my answers—including this one—and nothing changes, then I'd probably wait a day or two to see if things improve. If they don't, then the next time Roberta calls, I'd pick up the extension phone and invite her over for coffee the following evening. Before she arrived, I would go out and buy a brand-new outfit so I'd feel more confident about being able	Man—when Jerry reads that I'm think-ing about talking to both of them together, he'll really not like that idea.
• When, where, under what circumstances?		
• Specify your actions.		But since he won't like it, maybe that'll make him feel more inclined to get what

Question 6: (cont.)	Answer:	Distracting Thoughts and Worries:
• Rehearse blame-free statement.	to hold my own in a contest with Roberta. After that I'd write down everything I wanted to say, and stand in front of a mirror practicing until I sounded kind but firm. An hour or so before she was to arrive, I'd tell Jerry I hope he agrees with what I say in front of Roberta. And I would tell him that even if he doesn't, I want him to nod his head silently and wait to talk about it until after she leaves	I'm trying to say by reading his copy of my written answers.

I hope so—because having to face off with Roberta and Jerry at the same time might just be the scariest idea I've ever had. |
| • Handle worries. • Rehearse again. | so I won't be humiliated. I will need to practice being calm and clear about this. | |

Outcome

Kim did, in fact, give Jerry a copy of her "edited" remarks. And ten days later, she told us what happened:

"I didn't know how Jerry would react to what I'd written. I was nervous the whole day after I gave him that envelope. I even stayed later than usual at work and took the long way home. Then I stood outside our apartment trying to make my face look like nothing was wrong. But the instant I put my key in the door, Jerry flung it open and pulled me into his arms. We stood like that for a few minutes, and then we went inside and sat down. I was so relieved and happy right then that I can't remember exactly what he said. I think it was something about how what I'd written had really gotten to him and that he hated to learn that I felt like I was in second place with him. Then he kissed me and said he loved me more than he'd loved anyone and that the real reason he takes Roberta's calls all the time isn't that he has romantic feelings for her. It's because he feels sorry for her and a little guilty about the way he ended things.

"I could tell he was sincere, and his words took the sting out of the things that had been upsetting me all this time. So I don't worry about her calls anymore. Sometimes I sit there and cuddle with him while he talks. Other times I go off and do my own thing. And the other day, I was just walking through the room when I heard him answer the phone and tell Roberta he only had ten minutes to talk to her. And he got off the phone in less than eight minutes! Yeah, I looked at my watch. I couldn't believe Jerry actually set some limits and followed through without us fighting about it first."

Observations

We think that Kim's willingness to so thoroughly answer Question 1(*What are my negative feelings?*) set the stage and led her to come up with an especially effective and satisfying plan of action.

As she looked beyond her obvious feelings of anger and frustration, Kim discovered that she also felt suspicious and insecure. Those are the kinds of emotions that can be especially difficult to acknowledge. However, by taking the time to dig beneath the surface and identify the fuller range of her intense, negative feelings, Kim was able to free herself from their hold and to prevent them from clouding her mind or limiting her thinking.

Finally, Kim's calm and well-thought-out answer to Question 4 (*How would I like things between us to be?*), really impressed us. By using the words, "I would like Jerry to understand how badly I feel when I see him choosing her over me, and I'd like him to reassure me that I'm the number-one woman in his life," Kim made her desire to strengthen her connection to Jerry and her sense of vulnerability touchingly clear. And if she left those words in the edited version that she gave to her husband, we imagine they touched him too.

Troubles on Memory Lane

This story is yet another example of how the basic questions help people settle their couples' disputes when their partners do not respond to their specific requests for change. In this case, Neal and Molly, who married three years ago, are at odds about the way Molly interacts with her former husband, Larry. Neal, too, has been married once before. Both of their "exes" have remarried. Molly's three children from her first marriage, ages eight to fourteen, live with Molly and Neal. Neal has two grown-and-married children from his first marriage. All of these people live within fifteen minutes of each other.

Neal grumbles:

"You'd think by now that both of us would know how to handle our ex-spouses without upsetting each other. I know how to do that. Molly doesn't. And that's my problem in a nutshell.

"Since we've been married, Molly's parents invite Molly, me, and the kids, along with her "ex" and his new wife for dinner once a month. Larry's parents do the same thing. So Molly and I spend a lot of evenings with Larry and his wife. And within the first five minutes of these encounters, Molly and Larry launch into one of their 'Hey, remember when?' strolls down memory lane that leave me out. I don't know how Larry's wife feels about this, but I am bored and sick of being left out. I want Molly to put a stop to those conversations.

"I've asked her to do so repeatedly. Each time she's given me this big sigh and said, 'I think those memories are good for the children to hear, and besides, what else is there to talk about with him?' She totally ignores how I feel."

With his jaw clenched, Neal continued, "I've had enough of their memory lane. I've tried interrupting them, changing the subject, or leaving the table. Nothing stops them. I'm about ready to tell her that if it happens one more time, I will stop going to any more of these family get-togethers. I don't care how important she thinks my being there is for the kids!"

Here are Neal's responses to the six basic questions:

Question 1: What are my negative feelings?

I'm *angry* at Molly and Larry. I *resent* being ignored. It *hurts* that Molly hasn't changed what's going on (*Replace or remove blaming words.*) ~~since I've asked her to do that after every one of these memory lane fiascos~~. I'm fed up and ready to take things into my own hands.

Question 2: What's the fairest way to describe the problem?

(*We are different.*) We are different when it comes to how to treat your current spouse when the old one is around. (*No blaming, explaining, or guessing words.)* ~~I do this better than Molly does.~~ *(What do we usually do?)* Usually, Molly and Larry discuss things that happened before I came into the picture. I don't like that. I have asked Molly to stop doing this, but she hasn't. I have tried a few things to get her to stop and they haven't worked. I am ready to just stop going to these dinners, and I expect that Molly won't like that one bit.

Question 3: Why do I want to work things out?

~~So I won't feel like a third wheel.~~ *(Focus on positive feelings and/or practical reasons.)* So I can enjoy evenings with the extended family and feel appreciated at the same time.

Question 4: How would I like things between us to be?

Since we all get together regularly, I'd like us to spend at least some of that time on all-inclusive activities so we can begin building new memories that I am a part of.

Question 5: How can I actually get that?

When I was a camp counselor years and years ago, we used to do things like put together scavenger hunts for whole groups of people. So maybe something like that would work here. *(When, where, under what circumstances?)* The next time we all get together at Molly's folks' house and before anyone has a chance to settle into a repeat production of how things always go, I could take charge of the way the evening plays out by organizing a scavenger hunt. I can call ahead and let my in-laws in on the plans and ask them to help me keep it a secret. That way I'd have two people already on my side. *(Handle worries.)* In order to separate Molly and Larry so they don't build new, exclusive memories, I'd organize it as a boys against girls scavenger hunt.

(Specify your actions.) To get everyone involved and enjoying the scavenger hunt—and to try to keep the dinner conversation more about the scavenger hunt and less about Molly and Larry's good old days, I'd explain in advance that Grandma and Grandpa will be the judges and that they'll announce the winning and second-placed teams and give out awards after dinner.

Question 6: And if that doesn't work, what else can I do?

Call Larry and ask him and his wife to sit down with Molly and me. Then I'd just explain things to everyone involved and see if one of them can come up with a suggestion. I'd hate to do it this way because Molly and I could end up having an argument right in front of Larry, which would be embarrassing but not as bad as it feels to me when I am sitting around with these same people and feeling left out.

Outcome

When Neal called us several weeks later, he was delighted with how things had turned out. Here's what he said:

"Everyone liked the scavenger hunt. It went so well that Molly wants me to help her with an idea she has for next time. She wants to set up another competition. This one will help her parents. One team will clean Grandma's and Grandpa's attic, and the other team will clean their basement. First team done (with cleanliness in mind as judged by Molly and me) can choose between an afternoon of baking with Grandma or an afternoon of fishing with Grandpa. The second place team gets the other prize."

Observations

This story demonstrates how applying your answers to the questions in creative ways can produce satisfying end-results even when your partner won't cooperate. In this instance, Molly never did respond to Neal's direct request. Rather than remaining stuck or escalating things, Neal found another route to take that helped him achieve his goal.

Truth or Consequences

Jonathon is a recently remarried friend of ours. Following a contentious divorce and custody fight for their son, Noah, he and Nancy, his wife of six years, dissolved their marriage. Jonathon dated a number of different women for a while after that. Ten months ago he married Honey, a soft-spoken woman seven years younger than him who had not previously been married. As you read Jonathon's story, you will see how his written responses helped him get past his reluctance to solve the problem with what truly was the best and most obvious solution.

Noah is now five years old and enjoys spending every other weekend and some holidays with Honey and Jonathon. They like that arrangement as well. And when we see Honey and Jonathon out together, they look happy and very much in love. But apparently, it isn't all bliss for the newlyweds.

"Not by a long shot!" Jonathon informed us. "Honey is mad at me because I want her to cool it with my ex-wife. And I'm frustrated with her because she's too damned friendly with that witch.

"Remember when Nancy started pumping people for information about my lifestyle, my money situation, even how much I paid my secretary? Then she used every little scrap of information she could dig up as grounds to haul me into court and 'revisit' our financial settlement. I'm still upset about what happened!

"I've asked Honey several times now not to say anything to Nancy about what we have, what we spend, what we do, or where we go. But Honey rolls her eyes at me and says I'm paranoid and that 'my hostility has overtaken my brain,' which means she wants me to try and get along with Nancy for 'Noah's sake.' She thinks Nancy merely wants to make peace and be a good coparent. Hah! I don't understand why Honey can't see that Nancy's nothing but trouble!

"Maybe it's because she's never been married before, so she has no way to know firsthand how someone you thought you loved can turn into a vicious, backstabbing witch.

"If I wasn't worried about how she'd react, I'd tell Honey all the nasty details about what I had to go through to get my damn divorce. I wish Honey would just help me keep Nancy out of our lives. But Honey's a long way from doing that.

"In fact, when I woke up this past Saturday morning, I heard her laughing in the kitchen. I walked in there looking for coffee, expecting to find Honey enjoying something on TV and I froze—there sat Nancy acting all buddy-buddy with Honey.

"Honey smiled and turned in my direction to explain that Nancy had dropped Noah off early. And since it was so cold outside, she'd invited Nancy to sit down and have a cup of coffee before she headed back home. Behind her back, Nancy flashed her 'I gotcha' look, which propelled me right out of that room but not before I heard Nancy ask, 'Where did you buy those gorgeous slacks you're wearing, Honey—ooh, are they made of silk?'

"Later, after Nancy had left, I suggested that letting that witch into our house was like inviting a thief to do an inventory of our possessions. That made Honey so angry that she's barely spoken to me in three days.

"I don't know what to do. I've *got* to get Honey away from Nancy before we end up in the poor house!"

Since Jonathon was well acquainted with our work, he was very willing to try answering the basic questions. Take a look at his responses and the coaching cues that helped him below:

Question 1: What are my negative feelings?
(*Toward whom?*) *Worried* that Honey is going to end up giving Nancy information that she'll use against us in the future. *Irritated* with Honey because she won't do what I've asked, which is to stay away from Nancy.

Question 2: What's the fairest way to describe the problem?
(*We are different.*) We are different when it comes to how to treat my ex-wife. Honey trusts my ex-wife more than I want her to. (*No blaming, explaining, or guessing.*) ~~She refuses to believe me when I say Nancy's a witch. Probably because she sees only the good in people.~~ I've had bad experiences with Nancy, and I want to minimize our contact with her. I have not been able to get Honey to go along with me on this. Until I do, we have a problem.

Question 3: Why do I want to work things out?
I want to work this out so we won't end up getting screwed by my ex-wife.

Question 4: How would I like things between us to be?
I'd like us to stop fighting about this, and when we have to deal with Nancy, I want us to be polite, keep it brief, and say as little as possible.

Question 5: How can I actually get that?
How can I get Honey to limit her interaction with Nancy? I've tried everything

I can think of. (*Brainstorm if you're stuck.*) Although I'm not yet sure how to get what I want, I could try something this weekend because Noah won't be with us, so we can speak freely. There's one thing I could probably do, and I think it would work, but I can't bring myself to do it. I don't want to tell Honey how I caved in when Nancy threatened to talk with the business press. I'm not exactly proud that I agreed to pay a king's ransom in alimony every month rather than risk letting Nancy scare off potential investors in my new company by telling them just how underfinanced I was.

I'm concerned that if I tell Honey everything that happened, she'll be disappointed or disgusted by me. (*Handle worries.*) I suppose if she says or looks like she feels either of those things, I could say, "Whether you approve of what I did or not, I want you to know the whole story so that you'll understand why I need you to keep your distance from Nancy."

Question 6: And if that doesn't work, what else can I do?

I could have my attorney explain why he recommends we limit interactions with Nancy. Have him give her the down-and-dirty details of the deal I made in order to get out of that marriage. Hope I don't have to do this—but I will if all else fails.

Outcome

Within a few days, we learned what happened:

"After I used the 'brainstorm if you're stuck' coaching cue, I had to face the fact that telling Honey the whole story was what I needed to do, like it or not," Jonathon announced. "I was very embarrassed about my past actions, but it didn't make sense to let my pride keep me from doing the one thing I figured would work.

"But telling her was hard for me to do. Especially when I got to the part about how I agreed to say I had more money than I did, knowing that meant the judge would award Nancy an outrageous amount of alimony, all to keep her from frightening off potential investors in my new company.

"I hardly looked at Honey while I said most of that. When I finished, I apologized for having to go into all this with her. I said I'd been trying to protect her from any worry about business or money. I said that I wanted to continue to protect her and that to do that, I needed her stay away from Nancy!

"Honey said, 'You never told me why you were so hostile toward Nancy. I just assumed you were taking an unreasonably long time to get over your anger at her. Now that I know all the facts, I'll be much more careful about discussing anything that even approaches finances with Nancy. But I'll do it in a way that minimizes the chances of making things unpleasant for Noah.' And there you have it," Jonathon said with a smile. "What seemed like this enormous problem of mine just dissolved."

Observations

Jonathon's story makes two important points we would like you to notice. First, with the words, "I told her the whole story. Even the part about..." Jonathon summarized one of the most important things you can do when requesting specific actions from your partner: add in the background details about what led you to make this particular request. The more fully you share the details about things from your past that influence your thoughts and actions today, the more likely it is that the other person will be open and receptive to doing as you request or to suggesting another satisfactory approach.

Second, when Jonathon said, "This enormous problem of mine just dissolved," he reminded us that inviting a partner to help you formulate a plan (rather than imposing your own) is a great way to put the two you on the same side of the issue.

Thoughts to Take with You

When interactions with an ex-spouse put pressure on your marriage:
- Answer Question 1 thoroughly.
- Invite your spouse to help you come up with a plan.
- Add in details about what led you to make a specific request of your partner.

9

Relative Annoyances

Interfering parents, in-laws, and siblings

Family is that weird collection of people who have known you forever, seldom see you as an adult, and—for better or worse—will affect you for the rest of your life. And when you marry—that goes double!

Responding to the needs, requests, habits, idiosyncrasies, and expectations of two families (yours and your partner's) can be exhausting and confusing. It can even put your loyalty to the test. Well-intentioned or not, when family members comment on how you or your partner cooks, cleans, drives, parents, prays, handles money, and the like—their words can have a bruising effect on your marriage.

The stories you will find in this chapter come from two men and two women. Their words explain how they joined forces with their partners in order to limit the emotional impact of their well-meaning or not-so-well-meaning relatives.

Each person came up with a different solution. However, the key to their successes was identical. By tracking their answers to the basic questions, each found peaceful and productive ways to begin discussing the problem with their partner. What happened after that varied.

The Interrupting In-laws
What can you do if your in-laws are the source of your marital conflict and your partner is unwilling to confront them? The purpose of this story is to show you how asking and answering the basic questions can move you safely and effectively beyond such an impasse.

Recently, a young woman named Denise, her husband, Donald, and their newborn baby moved into JacLynn's neighborhood. Soon after, JacLynn and Denise began going for walks while Denise's in-laws baby-sat. One morning, JacLynn mentioned how nice it must be for Denise to have so much help from her husband's parents. Denise shrugged and said:

"I know I should be grateful to Donald's parents for all their help. And I am—but it's complicated. You see, we borrowed the money for the down payment on our new house from them, and they aren't charging us any interest. At first, I was thrilled at their generous offer to loan us the money, but now I'm not so sure it was a good idea because we feel so obligated to them that we're letting them do things we'd never have put up with before.

"They come over all the time without even calling first. They just barge in with their friends to give tours of our new home or to show off their first grandchild. They don't call or even knock first—they just walk right in on me and the baby! Since I'm shy about people watching me breast-feed, this whole thing makes me miserable.

"But because we owe them so much money, Donald won't tell them to stop. I think he's afraid of making them angry. So am I, but we have to do something about their interruptions because I'm a wreck."

"Could you sit down and talk to your in-laws about this?" JacLynn asked her.

"I thought about that, but I'm afraid of damaging our relationship. I just keep hoping that the newness of the baby will wear off soon and that they'll stop being so intrusive. I don't want to make waves if I don't have to. I really want Donald to speak to his folks about this, and I told him so, but so far he hasn't. Got any suggestions?"

Since, as a new mom, Denise was especially pressed for time, JacLynn just gave her a list of the basic questions and the coaching cues to take home overnight.

Here are Denise's written responses, which she shared with JacLynn the following day:

Question 1: What are my negative feelings?

I am *exhausted* and *weepy*—probably post-partum; *annoyed* at my in-laws for walking in on me without calling; *angry* at myself for feeling that way because they're really good to us; *disappointed* that Donald hasn't stepped in to protect me; *afraid* he never will; *scared* this situation will only get worse.

Question 2: What's the fairest way to describe this problem?
We borrowed the down payment on our house from Donald's parents. Now we feel obligated to them. When they come over unannounced to show off our house and their new grandchild, I get angry and nervous. I want Donald to ask his parents to call first. But he doesn't want to rock the boat, so he hasn't.

Question 3: Why do I want to work things out?
So I can enjoy my in-laws' visits instead of resenting them for popping over unannounced and so I can stop resenting Donald for letting this go on.

Question 4: How would I like things between us to be?
I'd like us to come to some kind of understanding with his parents. I'd like Donald to stand up to them and lay down some rules about when they can come over to visit and about calling us first.

Question 5: How can I actually get that?
To get Donald to talk to his parents, I guess I could try to explain again how uncomfortable it is for me when they stop by without checking to see if it's a good time or not. And again, I could ask Donald to talk with them about calling beforehand.

Question 6: And if that doesn't work, what else can I do?
On Friday nights we have dinner with Donald's parents, and the baby usually sleeps until we finish eating. Next Friday, maybe I could tell them that our pediatrician wants me to start getting the baby on a definite schedule. I could tell them he said I should block out certain hours everyday when no one comes by so I can get the baby used to a set routine. Then I could ask if they'd mind not coming over until after 6:30 P.M. (that way Donald would be home to help me cope with his parents and their friends).

I know it's not great to blame it on our pediatrician, but it would keep my in-laws from thinking Donald and I don't want them around.

Outcome

After JacLynn read Denise's written answers, Denise told her:

"Well, I *tried* to discuss this with Donald, but we got into a fight. You should have heard us; we sounded like a couple of scared babies. He said, 'If it bothers you that much then *you* bring it up!' And I shot back, 'They're *your* parents, you bring it up!' Then we both started laughing at what chickens we were.

"I told Donald about your six questions and said that since we owed his parents so much money, I figured he wouldn't want to confront them. I told him I'd thought of another plan, but it meant I'd be telling his parents a lie and I hated to do that. I showed him my answer to Question 6. Donald thought it was sneaky, but he said it was something I could probably pull off.

"'*Me*? What about *you*?' I said. 'I don't want to upset your folks any more than you do!' We started bickering again, and woke the baby.

"Donald said, 'Hey, what if we blame the baby?'

"I had no idea what he was talking about, so I just went on upstairs to take care of the baby. When I came back, Donald was waving a piece of paper with crayon writing all over it. He said, 'I got it! The solution really is to blame the baby. Take a look.' I read what he'd written and started giggling—luckily so did his parents when they read it.

"Here it is:

Dear Grandma and Grandpa,

My parents are too chicken to tell you this, so I'm doing the dirty work for them. I hope you won't be mad, but Mommy and Daddy want to know if you'd please start calling before you come over to see me. They love seeing you (so do I!), but they also love having time to get themselves and me dressed before you get here. They might never have told you this 'cause they love you, appreciate how you helped them buy a new house for me to grow up in, and they are afraid of hurting your feelings. They'd rather err on the side of safety and say nothing. But I said you'd understand. And they finally agreed with me because everyone knows—to "heir" is human!

Observations

This is one of those stories that didn't end as the person planned—it ended better than that!

In this case, Denise's effort to come up with a back-up plan—and her choice to share that plan with Donald—inadvertently set the stage for a surprising solution they both could live with.

What Am I? Chopped Liver?

Elliot, a man in his late twenties, had been married only seven weeks when he complained that he and his wife, Dana, were fighting all the time. As he put it, "Dana is an only child who would rather talk to her parents than spend time with me!" Elliot's tale shows another way to move forward when your spouse will not cooperate.

Here's Elliot's story:

"Ever since Dana and I got back from our honeymoon, we've been arguing repeatedly and heatedly about her family. Our latest fight happened last night. Just as we were leaving for the movies, Dana's mother called. Dana and her mother started talking about how they could get Dana's father to go to the doctor for a checkup. Their conversation dragged on and on. I kept pointing to my watch and mouthing the words, 'Tell her you'll call her later. We're going to be late!' But she ignored me.

"By the time Dana finally got off the phone, it was too late to go to the movie. Instead, we spent the night fighting. I told her that it was just one more example of her putting her family ahead of me. I even shouted, 'What am I? chopped liver? Don't my feelings count?' And then Dana said it was wrong for me to ask her to cut her mother's conversation short and that it would be rude of her to tell her mom that she had to hang up when her mother was so worried about her dad."

Below you will see how Elliot developed an effective, step-by-step plan to take the lead and alter the dynamics of his problem in a loving and positive manner. The seeds of his plan are contained in his responses to Questions 2, 4, and 5 below.

Question 2: What's the fairest way to describe the problem?

We disagree about how to handle phone calls from my in-laws. I think it's fine for Dana to talk with her parents but not when it cuts into our time together. (*No blaming, explaining, or guessing.*) ~~Dana acts like her parents come first.~~ (*Remove phrases implying you're stuck.*) ~~I can't get her to put me first, and I may not be able to do this, which spells bad news for the future.~~ (*What do we usually do?*) If her parents call during meals, or while we're sleeping, making love, or about to leave the house, I roll my eyes, gesture for Dana to hang up, or suggest we try leaving the phone off the hook for a change. Then Dana gets upset, starts to cry, and says we can't do that because she's all her parents have.

Question 4: How would I like things between us to be?

Unless there is an emergency involving her parents, I'd like Dana and her parents to arrange more convenient times to talk by phone. (*Specify your partner's realistic actions.*) And if they call when we are in the middle of doing something together, I'd prefer that Dana would say she'll call them back later.

Question 5: How can I actually get that?

I won't ask Dana to shorten or reschedule her conversations with her parents because I've done that many times and it hasn't worked. So I think I should try something else. Maybe I can phone her parents instead of waiting for them to call us. I can choose a convenient time when we aren't in the middle of doing something—and then call them myself. (*When, where, under what circumstances?*) Weeknights, between when I get home and when we eat dinner, I can call them and find out how they're doing.

When I finish my conversation, I can say, "We've got another half hour until we eat dinner, would you like to talk to Dana?" and then I can hand the phone to Dana. (*Keep your goal in mind.*) That way, we'd be able to catch up with what's new in her parents' lives, get off the phone before dinner, and have plenty of time to ourselves.

And I can do this on weekends if we have plans to go out for the evening so that Dana can take her time speaking with her folks and we can still be on time for whatever plans we have made.

Question 6: And if that doesn't work, what else can I do?

I can invite her parents over to talk about how we can make sure we stay closely in touch with them. And I can say that talking with them by phone is so important to Dana that she will stop anything else she is doing when they call. Then I can ask them to help me come up with a way to balance the desire to talk with them with my wish for uninterrupted meal times and also when we are heading out for a social event.

Outcome

Two weeks after Elliot wrote out his answers to the questions, he told us:

"After I saw you, I started phoning my in-laws each evening before dinner. Then after talking with them for a few minutes, I handed the phone to Dana. After about six days of this, Dana said, 'I don't get it. Why are you being so nice to my parents? I thought you hated them.'

"It turns out Dana had interpreted my wanting her to cut those calls with her parents short as my dislike of her parents. I have now convinced her that I genuinely like her folks, which is true. Dana said that when I tried to motion her to hang up the phone, she felt she had to stay on the phone just to let me know that even though she was married to me her parents were important, and she was not about to cut them out of her life.

"That took me by surprise. And apparently, my belief that she preferred spending time with her folks to spending time with me took her by surprise. Now that things are straightened out, Dana calls her folks before dinner, and then after a while she hands the phone to me."

Observations

Acting on his assumption that Dana "would rather talk to her parents than spend time with me," Elliot used the basic questions to come up with a goodwill plan of action that called for him to change his own behavior. And when he did phone her parents instead of waiting for them to call, he took the pressure to change off of Dana and eliminated the source of their conflict.

As an unexpected bonus, when Elliot began initiating phone calls to his in-laws, he was astonished to hear Dana say out loud for the first time what she'd assumed was true, "I thought you hated them." After that, Dana and Elliot found and took a direct approach to clearing up other assumptions each had made.

You May Be Right, Dear

The story below shows how answering the six questions helps people whose conflicts cannot be resolved to accept what is true, marshal their own resources, and come up with a solid back-up plan that leads to a satisfying conclusion. In this instance, Robert, a man in his late thirties, describes the negative impact that his brother and sister-in-law's divorce is having on his own marriage.

"My brother and sister-in-law are getting a divorce after nineteen years of marriage. My wife, Sharon, and I are very close to the both of them. Now we are so caught up in the drama of their divorce that we're fighting about it. I think my brother is right to end his marriage. Sharon disagrees. Our arguments are getting out of hand. Neither of us seems able to stop."

Robert chose to answer the basic questions in hopes of finding a way to disentangle himself from further disputes about his brother's divorce. His written responses follow:

Question 1: What are my negative feelings?

Angry at my sister-in-law. *Uneasy* when Sharon starts taking her side. *Annoyed* at Sharon that she doesn't see that my brother is doing the right thing. *Tired* of ending up in a fight about this. *Worried* that this is hurting our marriage.

Question 2: What's the fairest way to describe the problem?

Sharon and I have been close to my brother and his wife for many years. They are getting divorced. Sharon blames my brother. I don't. When I stick up for him, Sharon gets angry. We argue about this a lot. I have tried to get Sharon to stop mentioning the divorce at all, but this has not worked. Things are tense between us.

Question 3: Why do I want to work things out?

So we ~~don't end up dissolving our marriage, too.~~ (*Focus on positive feelings and/or practical reasons.*) will remain solid whether or not we agree about how my brother and his wife are conducting themselves.

Question 4: How would I like things between us to be?

(*Turn what you* don't *want into what you* do *want.*)   I would like ~~my wife and me to stop fighting about this. And since my brother is getting a divorce, I would like to be able to stand by him without having to argue about it with my wife and without it hurting my marriage and~~ for Sharon to accept my choice to support my brother even if she disagrees with me. (*What would the perfect partner do?*) The perfect partner would tell me she understands that I feel loyal to my brother. And if she believed that my brother was to blame for his own situation, she would simply say, "I love you for being so true to your family."

Question 5: How can I actually get that?

The only way to get Sharon to stop arguing is to agree with her, but I can't do that this time. My loyalty to my brother is on the line. (*Keep your goal in mind.*) In order to have Sharon accept my choice to stand by my brother even though she disagrees with me, I guess I could refuse to talk about the divorce. But I don't know how long I could keep quiet if Sharon keeps bringing it up, which she's likely to do.

(*Specify your actions.*) Maybe instead of refusing to discuss things at all, I could say, "You may be right, dear." But that's not going to be enough to keep her from arguing the point. (*Handle worries.*) I'd have to add something like, "I love you very much, and even though we disagree, I hope you can respect my need to stand by my brother."

(*When, where, under what circumstances?*) I could say that the next time she brings it up. I think this is a lot better than arguing or refusing to talk about things. Plus, it will feel better to have a nice way to ask her to ease off.

Question 6: And if that doesn't work, what else can I do?

Go back to my "refusing to discuss this" idea. It's not a perfect solution, but it works sometimes. And sometimes is better than not at all.

Outcome

Robert found that by combining the words, "You may be right, dear," with, "I love you very much and even though we don't agree, I hope you can respect my need to stand by my brother right now," he was able to call a halt to their arguing. He also told us how much Sharon appreciated hearing him say, "I love you very much."

"She said hearing that is what gave her the courage to tell me that she was worried about whether our marriage was as strong and healthy as she hoped it would be. And suddenly, there we were, both of us pointing out how our marriage was stronger than my brother and sister-in-law's.

"I think that worrying about whether our marriage would end in divorce may have been what was going on underneath the surface of our arguments. Whether that's true or not, I'm glad we both feel good about our marriage."

Observations

Using phrases like, "You may be right, dear," acknowledges (rather than dismisses as "wrong") the other person's position and it helps to reduce the quarrelsome nature of a dispute. When you add in words to reassure your partner of your tender feelings toward him or her like, "I love you very much," and follow that with a direct request, such as "and even though we disagree, I hope you can respect my need to stand by my brother," you make it easier for both of you to focus on your shared relationship and hang in there together despite your disagreements.

In this case, when Robert uttered those words, he implied that the issue of *who* was right or wrong was clearly less important than *how* they felt about one another. And that helped both of them relax and move on to other topics of discussion.

The Buffer Zone

When Amy, a woman in her late fifties whose mother-in-law criticized her frequently, was called upon to become her caretaker, she wanted her husband to defend her from his mother's verbal attacks. Based on her unsuccessful efforts to get that in the past, Amy doubted her husband would stand up to his mother now. She was amazed and delighted to discover that by paying close attention to her written responses to the basic questions, there was another avenue open to her that could (and did) lead to equally satisfying results.

This is her story:

"I can never please that woman," she told us. "From the minute Brian and I got married thirty-nine years ago, his mother has been critical of me. At first she said things to me like, 'You call that cooking?' Or, 'Maybe you just never learned to iron correctly.' Then her attacks became even more deliberate: 'You're the worst housekeeper I have ever seen.'

"I used to try to get Brian to stand up for me, but all he ever did was say, 'I know it's hard, but she doesn't mean any harm. She's just overprotective.'

"Brian and his mother are quite close because his father was killed in Vietnam. Still, I think he should have defended me. But after so many years, I gave up and simply limited my contact with her. I would see her on holidays or family occasions, but mostly Brian would see her on his own. Recently, however, she broke her hip and needed someone to monitor her medications, clean house, and fix meals. And I got the job because Brian works full time. Now we're right back where we started.

"She refuses to eat what I cook, and she hates the way I clean. Brian says he appreciates what I am doing, but still, he stands by and lets her light into me. Something has to be done!"

Question 1: What are my negative feelings?

Angry at my husband for not getting his mother to stop berating me and for not protecting me from her nastiness. *Angry* at my mother-in-law for her verbal abuse of me. *Angry* at myself for letting her comments get to me.

Question 2: What's the fairest way to describe the problem?

Brian's mother makes nasty comments about everything I do. Usually I stay away from her, but now she's bedridden and needs someone to cook and clean and dole out her medicines at the right time. I am the only family member available to do this, so I've taken it on, but I am unhappy with the way she treats me. I want Brian to protect me from his mother's words. Brian wants me to overlook her remarks. I have tried, but I can't seem to do that.

Question 3: Why do I want to work things out?

So that when I am confronted with my mother-in-law's unpleasant taunts, I can feel as though I have some support and feel less alone.

Question 4: How would I like things between us to be?

I would like us to handle this problem together. I'd like Brian to do something to buffer me from his mother's comments while I take care of her.

Question 5: How can I actually get that?

Since Brian isn't going to get his mother to stop being mean to me, maybe he would distract his mother or keep her busy while I am over there cooking or cleaning so she'd be too busy to criticize me. I could ask Brian about this tonight. See if he has any ideas about how the two of us could keep me out of line of fire.

Question 6: And if that doesn't work, what else can I do?

Go and talk to her priest? See if her church has volunteer "visitors" who could be there during the days and hours I am there to clean and care for her? I think that would help because my-mother-in-law probably would tone down her comments in front of other people. And even if she didn't, I imagine the visitors would try to distract her. This wouldn't be as good as having Brian there to help me, but I think it would be better than things are now.

Outcome

Three weeks later, Amy told us that she had asked Brian to help "buffer" her and that he was immediately willing to do that. Since then, she said that the two of them had been having a grand time coming up with new ways to thwart his mother's ability to complain. Among the things they tried: telling the mother-in-law that they'd both had a hand in preparing her meals (which left her afraid to complain in case she hurt her son's feelings).

What Amy made clear was that whether the things she and Brian planned worked or not, the fact that they were doing this together made her feel less lonely and more connected to her husband.

Observations

Amy's story illustrates the benefits of carefully rereading your answers to the questions before you move on to the next one. Her words describe this best:

"I hoped that answering the basic questions would show me a new way to get Brian to defend me. But I didn't find anything new or helpful until I reread my answer to Question 4 (*How would I like things between us to be?*). I noticed that I'd written the word *buffer*. And that's when it occurred to me that asking Brian to buffer or shield me from his mother's behavior would be different from asking him to defend me. Buffering me would be something we could plan to do together. And the idea that we could do something like that together made me feel better."

Thoughts to Take with You

When dealing with "Relative Annoyances" it can be helpful to:
- Reassure your partner that you love him or her.
- Look back at your answers for clues about new ways to settle things in your answers.

10

Parents. Partners. Problems.

Bringing up your kids without bringing down your marriage

Decisions about the discipline, education, and lifestyle of children provide husbands and wives with plenty of opportunity for conflict—and plenty of chances to strain their marriages. When parents disagree about how to raise their children, what do they do? Generally, they fight, they fold, or they flee.

Of course, it doesn't take long to figure out that fighting, folding, or fleeing produces neither healthy parents nor happy partners. And after they've made that discovery for themselves, people often tell us they feel torn between their desire to be a good parent and their wish to be a loving spouse.

The purpose of this chapter is to show you that it's possible to be both of those things at the same time. Here, you will watch how two women and one man, whose children range in age from nine to twenty-three, handle disputes with their spouses about how to answer a teen daughter's probing questions, select the best treatment for a youngster with learning disabilities, and respond when a young-adult son declares that he is gay.

As you read each couple's answers to the six basic questions, you will see that these people felt calmer, stopped viewing their partners as the enemy, and found themselves acting more kindly toward their mates. You'll also notice that while their separate positions about how to raise the kids didn't necessarily change, these people came up with some great ways to disagree while holding hands with their partners.

Mom, Dad, Did You Ever Do Drugs?

This is a story about a couple who found themselves stuck in a dispute about when, how, and whether to reveal their past behaviors to their fourteen-year-old daughter. As you read it, you'll see that this account demonstrates an interesting and effective way for you to move ahead with your partner even if he or she will not agree to handle things your way.

Kathy and David have been married for seventeen years. Their daughter, Megan, is a typical teen who hangs out with a nice but odd-looking group of kids, some of whom have pierced noses and strangely colored hair.

Here's how Kathy described her problem:

"David and I have been arguing ever since last week when Megan asked us whether or not we'd ever done drugs. I had just opened my mouth to tell her that like a lot of other baby boomers, yes, I'd experimented a few times and luckily I didn't suffer some of the long-term side effects that several of my friends did. But before I could say that, David lifted me out of my chair, helped me into my coat, and asked Megan, 'Mind if we talk about this later? I want to take your mother out for coffee while you finish up your homework.'

"Ten seconds after that I was sitting in the car sputtering, 'David, what's wrong with you? What's this about going out for coffee all of a sudden?'

"'You were just about to tell Megan the truth! I had to do something fast,' he said.

"'So what? We never lie to any of our kids. You know that,' I replied.

"'Well, it's time we change that procedure. If Megan asks again, I want you to tell her you've never tried drugs. And that's what I'm going to do too.'

"'No way,' I told him. 'I'm not going to pretend that I've never come up against the same issues and pressures from my friends that she's facing. I want to tell her what happened so she'll make different and smarter choices.'

"'Kathy, that's like giving her permission to do drugs. She'll hold it over our heads from now on and say, "You can't tell me not to do drugs—you did them yourself when you were my age."'

"'David, I am not going to lie about this to Megan. I want her to trust me enough to be able to ask me any question she has, and I want her to know that I'm not like some of those other parents out there who are so out of touch with what their kids are going through that they're clueless about how to advise them.'

"'Meaning you think that's how Megan sees me?' he demanded.

"Then I said, 'Yes, as a matter of fact!'

"You get the picture. We bickered like that for the rest of the night. And ever since then, David and I have been arguing about everything that requires us to make a decision on behalf of Megan or the other kids."

Kathy's written responses to the basic questions follow:

Question 1:	Answer:	Distracting Thoughts and Worries:
What are my negative feelings?	**Offended** David challenged me on this because he's always known where I stand on the issue of telling the truth to our kids. **Angry** that he still doesn't see the danger in lying.	David's an idiot! How can he not know that when you lie to your kids, they sense it? Lie to them, and they'll start to distrust you. I am determined to win this. This is too important for me to give in.
Question 2:	Answer:	Distracting Thoughts and Worries:
What's the fairest way to describe the problem? • We are different.	We are different when it comes to how much of our pasts to reveal to our children. When kids ask, I believe the truth is always the right way to respond. David believes telling the truth, especially in this case, is a bad idea. He thinks Megan will use it against us. We're quarreling. I'd like to stop without giving in to David, but I don't know how to do that.	I know what it's like to grow up in a house full of lies—eventually it breaks your heart. Well, I won't let that happen, even on a small scale, to my kids.

Question 3:	Answer:	Distracting Thoughts and Worries:
Why do I want things to work out? • Focus on positive feelings and/or practical reasons.	~~Normally, I just do what I think is best and worry about how to get around David's objections later, but~~ it would be so much better if we could handle any kind of question from the kids without ~~getting bent out of shape with each other or~~ having our conflicts push us apart or "turning off" the kids.	We need to settle this because the older they get, the more heavy-duty, personal questions our kids are going to have.

Question 4:	Answer:	Distracting Thoughts and Worries:
How would I like things between us to be? • Turn what you **don't** want into what you **do** want. • Specify your partner's realistic actions.	When we get upset about the kids, I would like to be able to talk things out calmly ~~without getting upset with each other or arguing~~. If David doesn't want to tell Megan the truth, then I'd like him to tell her that he's not going to answer her question but that he **will** talk to her about what he knows and worries about when it comes to drugs and her ability to make really good, informed decisions. And I'd like David to stay there with me while I tell Megan about my personal experience with drugs.	I get that David is fine with keeping secrets from the kids, but I'm not and I never will be! I'd feel better if David would sit there with me while I tell Megan my story, but I don't want to make him feel like he's just a bump on a log.

Question 5:	Answer:	Distracting Thoughts and Worries:
How can I actually get that? • Keep your goal in mind. • When, where, under what circumstances?	How can I talk calmly to David about this without us getting upset? There's no guarantee this will work, but I can probably call him now and ask him to meet me for coffee after work so we can talk before we go home.	Meg's going to ask again soon. I can't put off answering her again. The longer it takes to work this out, the more worried I get about what's going on in Megan's head.
• Specify your actions. • Rehearse blame-free statement.	When we meet, I can begin by saying, "David I love you very much, and I know we both want Megan to make good decisions for herself." Then I can tell him that I want to blend our two ways of dealing with her question into one approach, and what I'd like to try is for us to sit down with Megan when we go home. I can tell David that the first thing I would do is say to Megan that we're both worried about making sure she doesn't turn my past mistakes into permission to do the same thing because that's not okay with either one of us. I would say that her father would rather I didn't answer her question but that I am going to take a chance and trust her with the truth if she'll assure us that she will not	As much as I love David, I wish I didn't have to deal with him while I'm so worried for Meg.

Question 5: (cont.)	Answer:	Distracting Thoughts and Worries:
	mimic my mistakes nor share what I've told her with anyone, including her siblings or friends.	I don't want Megan to blab this to her friends—it's not something I'm proud of and it's private.
• Handle worries.	And to keep David from feeling like a bump on a log, I would tell him I'd like him to keep an eye on things. And if he finds I am giving Megan too much information or if he senses that she will turn what I've said into an excuse to experiment with drugs, I would like him to say so immediately.	

Question 6:	Answer:	Distracting Thoughts and Worries:
And if that doesn't work, what else can I do?	If David won't try my idea or come up with one of his own, then I guess I can go ahead and answer Megan privately. That won't solve things between David and me, but it will settle things for the moment with Megan. Then I can invite a few of Meg's friends' parents over for dinner and ask them to tell David and me how they've settled problems like this.	What I just wrote makes me really want to talk to Meg with David instead of by myself. Even if he doesn't say a word while I talk with Meg, his presence would give me some back-up if her questions got too difficult for me.

Outcome

Kathy met with David that evening and, just as she'd written in her answer to Question 5 (*How can I actually get that?*), the first thing she told him was, "David, I love you very much, and I know we both want to help Megan make good decisions for herself." Here's what Kathy said happened after that:

"David listened to everything I had to say. Then he told me that he didn't like what I wanted to do, but he'd rather be there when I talked to Meg so he could jump in and help if things started to get out of hand. So that night, the three of us sat down together just like I'd planned. When we finished talking, Megan hugged us both, said thanks, and told us we were 'cool.'

"David and I smiled at each other and relaxed for a mini-heartbeat when Megan said she wanted to be a cool parent just like us but that she definitely did not want to be as old as we were when she had kids.

"'But I was only twenty years old when you were born,' I gasped.

"'Exactly,' she replied, over the sounds of David's groan."

Observations

We especially like this story because it demonstrates what can happen when, instead of automatically discounting your partner's different opinion or choice you begin your discussion by *expressing* your positive feelings toward your partner, *identifying* things you both want to teach your children (like respect for others, personal safety, etc.), and *exploring* ways to do that together.

In this case, Kathy laid out exactly how she would do that when she wrote, "I can begin by saying, 'David, I love you very much, and I know we both want Megan to make good decisions for herself.' Then I can tell him that I want to blend our two ways of dealing with her question into one approach and..."

Clearly, when you start from that position, it becomes easier for both people to consider and be open to trying new ways to get somewhere together.

Ritalin, Rumors, and Rancor

This is a story about Melissa, Nate, and their nine-year-old daughter, Hannah, who recently was diagnosed with Attention Deficit Hyperactivity Disorder (ADHD). Melissa wants to get her daughter started on Ritalin, a drug that has produced good results in many ADHD children. Nate is strongly opposed to that. He believes pharmacology is too dangerous.

Here's how Melissa sees things:

"I've met with Hannah's teachers, her doctor, and a specialist. Everyone thinks we should try her on Ritalin, which they say is one of the most powerful tools for children with ADHD. But Nate, who knows almost nothing about ADHD and is suddenly a self-declared expert, says, 'Common-sense measures, such as getting a good night's sleep, eating well, and keeping unnecessary stresses to a minimum, help children with ADHD to feel and function better.'

"To which I say, 'Duh…eating well and sleeping right helps anybody with any kind of problem, but it isn't enough help for ADHD! I want to get Hannah started on Ritalin now—Hannah's doctor recommends it.'

"Nate wants to hold off and try other things like homeopathy, magnets, sound or visual training, megavitamins, yeast eradication, etc.

"Meanwhile, Hannah's struggling in school and has very few friends. Her self-image is hurting. The longer we take to decide what to do, the longer Hannah's problem goes untreated. The doctor says without treatment, children can get so much negative feedback that they start to think that they are bad or stupid. I am at my wit's end trying to get Nate to stop holding us back."

As you watch Melissa work her way through the six questions, we'd like you to notice how valuable she found it to read over her words before moving on to the next question:

Question 1:	Answer:	Distracting Thoughts and Worries:
What are my negative feelings?	**Furious** at Nate for acting like he doesn't trust my ability to decide on a safe treatment plan for Hannah. **Impatient** to help her. **Irritated** that Nate's dragging his feet on this.	Hannah needs attention **now**! I know more about what's going on and what is most likely to work than Nate. And even if Ritalin doesn't work, at least we will have tried something instead of wasting time arguing about what to do.

Question 2:	Answer:	Distracting Thoughts and Worries:
What's the fairest way to describe the problem? • We are different. • What do we usually do?	We are different when it comes to trusting physicians and their recommendations. The doctors want to put Hannah on Ritalin. I agree. Nate doesn't. He wants to try alternative medical treatments. We're barely talking to one another because of this. While we disagree, nothing is being done for Hannah.	I spend more time with Hannah and I get all the calls from school about her bad behavior, etc., so why shouldn't I know more about all of this than he does? Nate seems more concerned about being right than about doing the right thing for her!

Question 3:	Answer:	Distracting Thoughts and Worries:
Why do I want to work things out?	So we can stop arguing and help Hannah!	Nate needs to get off his high horse about how inferior Western medicine is.

Question 4:	Answer:	Distracting Thoughts and Worries:
How would I like things between us to be? • Specify your partner's realistic actions.	I'd like us to remember that Hannah is the priority here, not which one of us wins or whether one treatment is better than another. Specifically, I'd like Nate to arrange for Hannah to spend the night with his parents. Then when we're alone, I'd like him to say, "I'm sorry we've been fighting. I know Hannah needs us to help her, and I'd like us to do that together. You've met with her doctors already, but would you go back again with me? I want to ask my own questions, and then we can figure things out from there."	

Question 5:	Answer:	Distracting Thoughts and Worries:
How can I actually get that?	I could arrange for Hannah to spend Friday night with Nate's folks. Then, when we are alone, I'd hug him, pour us both a glass of wine, and then say to Nate, "Repeat after me: 'Melissa, I don't like that we've been at each other about what's best for Hannah. I know she needs to start some sort of treatment right away, and I'd like us to figure out what to do together. I know you've already met with a lot of people about this, but could we go back and talk with them together so I could ask my own questions and then figure things out from there?'"	Nate's folks would love this. This is a lot like what I did to hurry him up about proposing to me, and it worked then so maybe it'll work again—at worst it'll give us a laugh.

Question 6:	Answer:	Distracting Thoughts and Worries:
And if that doesn't work, what else can I do?	Tell him that if he will come to the pediatrician's office, ask all the questions he has, and listen to what she says, and then if he still wants to try the holistic approach and if the doctor will monitor what we do, I'll go along with him on that.	

Outcome

Melissa's description of what happened next follows:

"After we talked, we agreed to go together to Hannah's doctor early the next week. By the time we left there, we'd settled on a treatment plan that Hannah's been on for the last three weeks. The jury's still out on whether this approach is working. If it's not, we'll try other things until we make progress.

"Answering the basic questions helped me get a handle on what we were fighting about. Reading what I'd written (especially my comments in the margin like, 'Nate needs to get off his high horse about how inferior Western medicine is,' and, 'Nate seems more concerned about being right than about doing the right thing for Hannah!') I saw that I'd been thinking of Nate as an obstacle to get around instead of as my husband and friend. I had lost sight of the fact that he loves Hannah as much as I do, and he has a right to his own set of worries and beliefs. Once I saw that, I calmed down, and my sense of 'fairness' came back to me. After that I started acting nicer and so did he."

Observations

While it seems like basic common sense to approach our partners with the positive feelings we have for them firmly in mind, in the heat of the moment that's a lot easier said than done. But as this story demonstrates, that's when answering the basic questions can really help. As Melissa put it:

"I found it odd that listing my angry feelings helped me to calm down. Then, reading some of my early answers showed me where my thinking about Nate was flawed and probably unreasonable. After that, my sense of 'fairness' automatically took over and I started acting nicer. Then so did Nate. And that nicer way of treating each other carried over to how we are making the decisions we've had to make on Hannah's behalf. I'm glad all this happened because now Nate and I feel like we're on the same side. That's a terrific feeling, and I think Hannah likes this change too."

Don't Ask. Don't Tell.

Murray and his wife, Joyce, are at odds over how to react to their twenty-three-year-old son, Kevin's recent revelation that he is gay.

Murray told us:

"Seems Kevin told his mother that he was gay before I found out. I discovered this two weeks later when I demanded to know what all the whispering and the sudden end of conversation when I came into the room was all about. I thought they'd hang their heads and sheepishly admit they were planning a surprise birthday party for me. Instead, I heard Kevin say the unthinkable: 'Dad, I'm gay.'

"On the outside, I stayed calm and unshaken, but inside my head everything I'd ever heard about homosexuality was flying around—insults like 'faggot,' 'queer,' and 'pervert' collided with my fears of AIDS. My feelings were too strong and confusing to handle.

"I walked out of the room—out of the house—and drove to my office. I spent the night on the couch there. The next day, I did not say a word to my son, but I unloaded on my wife. I blamed her for all the years she coddled him and even the time she let him learn to knit. I said some other unkind things too.

"Joyce didn't even try to talk to me until later when she begged me to say something to Kevin about loving him no matter what. I turned her down flat. But when she said someone had told her that kids whose parents were unbending in their disapproval were prone to suicide, I calmed down enough to go in and give my son a quick hug. I may have been in shock about his lifestyle, but the last thing I wanted was for him to think I hated him or to be so unhappy with the facts of his life that he saw death as the only way out.

"It's been over a month, and I feel like these are the most desperate and dark days of my life. It's hard to go on every day at work pretending to be okay. I do not want to tell anyone. Dealing with the normal questions you get from people asking, 'Has he got a girlfriend?' is a nightmare. I'm reeling from the blow.

"To make matters worse, my wife and I are hardly able to talk about it without anger and tears. I just wish this was all a bad dream and that I could wake up tomorrow morning to find that it is all gone."

Murray spent several days working on his personal answers to the basic questions. Sometime later, he agreed to let us share them with you here:

Question 1: What are my negative feelings?

Angry at Kevin, myself, Joyce, and God. *Disgusted* by Kevin. (Isn't homosexuality an unnatural perversion?) *Guilty*. Is this my fault? (Thinking about what I might have done or shouldn't have done.) *Worried* for my son about the hostility that homosexuals encounter. *Concerned* that he'll get AIDS or be lonely in his old age without a family of his own. *Sad* I'll never have grandchildren and that the family name ends here.

Question 2: What's the fairest way to describe the problem?

Joyce wants me to accept this and to think of Kevin the same way I did before he told me he was gay. I can't; it flies in the face of my religious convictions. My problem is not just about how terrible I feel about Kevin's disclosure but it's also driving a wedge between me and Joyce. We keep arguing about what the correct response is to this whole thing.

Question 3: Why do I want to work things out?

So I don't have to come home everyday and see my wife's disappointment or feel the distance that's come between me and my son.

Question 4: How would I like things between us to be?

I would like things to be calm. (*What would the perfect partner do?*) The perfect partner would give me more time to adjust. She'd say, "I know this comes as a shock to you," and, "I want you to know that you're not in this alone. I am right here with you." She'd also say she wants us to work through this together. Then she'd tell me that she'd taken it upon herself to assure Kevin that I love him and that she had asked him to give both of us however long we may need to adjust to all of this.

Question 5: How can I actually get that?

Usually, I can talk to Joyce about my problems. But this is just too difficult for me to talk about. The best I can manage is to write a few of my thoughts down and leave them for her to read in the morning. I'll explain in the note that I can't talk about this right now—that I am trying to get to the same place she is in terms of being more accepting of Kevin but that I need time and patience. And that I love them both very much.

Question 6: And if that doesn't work, what else can I do?

Continue to pray for guidance? Seek religious counseling? Ask Joyce and Kevin to give me some more time to adjust to all of this. Go to a bookstore and check to see if there are any books of advice for fathers who are in my situation.

Outcome

Months later, Murray recapped what happened after he answered the six questions.

Here is what he related to us:

"Eventually, I wrote a brief note to my wife. It said pretty much what I wrote down as my answer to the fourth question (*How would I like things between us to be?*). Melissa was wonderful. She did everything I'd said that a perfect partner would do. And she did one more thing—she gave a copy of my note to Kevin so that he would really know that I loved him even though I couldn't say that at the time.

"We didn't talk about any of this for a while. But we tried to act normally around one another. Kevin played along nicely. Then, last week, he wrote me a note inviting his mother and me to go with him to a PFLAG meeting. He didn't say what PFLAG was, and I didn't ask. But we went with him two nights ago, and it turned out to be a gathering of parents and friends of lesbians and gay people.

"I was taken aback by how normal all the people looked and how matter-of-fact they seemed to be about homosexuality. We met and talked with another couple there who we liked very much. They have *two* gay children. And they understood how hard this can be on parents. When the evening was over, I turned to Kevin and thanked him for bringing us to a place where we can relearn how to be proud parents of our fine (albeit gay) son and how to be the same old happily married couple we really are.

"Now I feel some relief. I am beginning to understand that Kevin told us about his being gay not to hurt us or to create distance but out of love and truth and a desire for honesty, intimacy, and closer communications—which is something he says he learned from me and his mom."

Observations

Sometimes you've just got to take time for yourself. Finding the words that can help you ask your partner for that time can be especially important when you are in emotional upheaval. In this story, we think that Murray did a remarkable job of turning what he'd written in his answer to Question 4 (*How would I like things between us to be?*) into an effective way to ask for the time he needed.

Thoughts to Take with You

Suggestions about bringing up the kids without bringing down your marriage:
- Start by expressing your loving feelings toward your partner then identify what you both want for your children.
- Reread your answer before moving on to the next question.
- Ask for and take some time for yourself.

11

Stepfamilies: When You've Stepped in It (and You Will!)

Making your way past the pressures and pitfalls of life in a blended family

---

This is a chapter for biological parents and stepparents whose love for one another is beginning to buckle in the face of the extraordinary pressures of stepfamily life. Currently, nearly three out of five families in this country are raising children from another parent, different marriages, and different families. These blended families include adopted children, divorced families raising children together, and children from other marriages or relationships.

Combining any number of "yours, mine, and ours" children under a single roof can be so stressful, exhausting, and unsettling that it can suck the life out of any romance. As one man put it, "You don't know what you don't know about how hard this is until you're under siege!"

In this chapter, there are two stories. One comes from a woman who is struggling to maintain a loving relationship with her new husband while she copes with their different parenting styles, the discomfort of divided loyalties, and the understandable urge to favor her own child. As you read along, you will see how she uses the basic questions to figure out where to begin. The second story, told from a man's point of view, describes the difficulty that people without children often experience when they become instant stepparents. We hope these stories will motivate you to look for creative and effective ways to meet the challenges and enjoy the rewards of building your own successful stepfamily.

And Now a Word from the Evil Stepmother

Living in a blended family can be overwhelming. At times, so many problems can crop up simultaneously that it can be hard to figure out what's going on. We selected the story you are about to read because we want to show you how one person managed to sort through her relationship problems and move beyond the chaos.

Joan is a woman in her mid-thirties. She had been divorced for five years when she met and fell in love with Michael, also in his mid-thirties. Like Joan, Michael had been married once before. Each had a child from a first marriage. Two years ago, Joan and Michael got married and moved into a new home with Joan's twelve-year-old daughter, Sarah. Michael's fourteen-year-old son, Ben, spends every other weekend, many holidays, and most of the summer with them.

According to Joan, "For the first few months, I thought, 'Finally, I'm part of a warm and loving family.' I was so happy—especially for Sarah.

"But after the newness wore off, things turned sour. They're so bad right now that I don't know what to do. Even how the dishes get scraped or when and where the kids do their homework has turned into a battle ground for Michael and me. And the kids fight with each other over everything—you name it.

"There's constant fighting. Michael picks on Sarah about every stupid thing from how fast she eats to what television shows she should be able to watch; then Michael and I argue about how he treats Sarah. Michael's son, Ben, and I argue too about the mess he makes around the house, like how he repeatedly leaves his clothes on the bathroom floor. Then there's the never-ending battle we have about whether to rent R-rated videos where, even when I try to reason with Ben, he calls me his 'evil stepmother,' races to his room, and slams the door.

"I asked Michael to come with me to couples' counseling because I am concerned about all of this, but he won't. He says he did the therapy thing with his first wife and that this time, if we have problems, we will just work them out together. I told him that sounded fine but that I had no idea how to do that. Michael didn't seem worried. He said to just 'Shake it off and forget it,' which is typical of how Michael deals with things. And it's just one more way he makes me feel like I'm alone in this marriage.

"Nothing has turned out the way I had hoped it would. As much as I love Michael—and I really do—I hate being a stepmother to Ben and I hate the kind of stepfather Michael is to Sarah. Giving it more time is not going to fix things. I'd like to try and improve things between Michael and me. But there is just too much that is wrong. We have so many problems all at once that I don't see how it's possible. I don't even know where to start anymore."

Before we asked Joan to write out her answers to the basic questions, we suggested that she read some of the stories in earlier chapters of this book.

Here is her reaction to the stories she read:

"It seemed like the people in those stories instantly came up with answers that were short and to the point, without a whole lot of trouble. I was worried I couldn't do that because I don't think as fast on my feet or as clearly as the people I read about did."

In case that is your reaction too, below you will find Joan's answers to the six questions, the coaching cues she used, and a description of what she was thinking and feeling as she moved from question to question.

Question 1:	Answer:	Distracting Thoughts and Worries:
What are my negative feelings? •Get rid of negative labels. • Toward whom? • Pay attention to all your negative feelings.	**Angry** at Michael for ~~acting like a know it all who's in charge of~~ disciplining Sarah. **Guilty** about feeling that way when I can see he's trying. **Afraid** marrying Michael was a huge mistake. **Concerned** that staying married is bad for Sarah. **Concerned** that leaving the marriage is bad, too, because it will show Sarah it's okay to run away from difficult problems.	All that answering this question is doing is making me more and more aware of all the reasons that I'm upset.

Question 1: (cont.)	Answer:	Distracting Thoughts and Worries:
• Eliminate **should/ shouldn't**.	Sometimes I **resent** Sarah ~~but I shouldn't~~ for not getting along with Michael and Ben. **Unhappy** about how disrespectful Ben is to me. **Furious** that Michael doesn't get Ben to stop. **Unsure** how to be a stepmother to a teenage boy. **Angry** at myself because, before I married Michael, I wish we had discussed how we would be as parents. **Tired. Depressed. Alone.**	

"Now that I've written out my first answer, I see that it only looks like people came up with instant answers, because while I was writing I was making other snap judgments in my head about past events compared to my present-day problems. For instance, I was flashing on how I don't like Ben leaving his muddy soccer shoes in the front hall and how Michael doesn't even notice the mess Ben makes. And how Michael doesn't like Sarah crawling into bed with us on Sunday mornings but I do; I love to cuddle with her then.

"I didn't write about those things in my answer, so you can't tell that they had any bearing on what I put down on paper. But they did."

Question 2:	Answer:	Distracting Thoughts and Worries:
What's the fairest way to describe the problem? • We are different.	We're different in what we think children and stepparents should and shouldn't do. I think I should be the primary disciplinarian with Sarah and he should be that with Ben. I think a stepparent should check with the biological parent before making rules. I don't like fighting about the kids. I don't like being an "evil stepmother". I'd like us to see a family therapist together but Michael won't.	Michael knows we have problems, but he just shrugs it off and says to give it more time.
• What do we usually do?	Whenever we talk about parenting, he acts like he disagrees with me. We argue. Then he says "give it more time." I don't think more time will make any difference. We disagree about that too.	I don't want to live like this. I don't want Sarah to think marriage is supposed to be like this.

"Writing an answer to this question didn't seem useful. All I did was write down the things I already knew. That didn't help me figure out what our problem was. But rereading was helpful because when I saw that I wrote, 'Michael acts as if he disagrees with me,' I realized that I wasn't one hundred percent sure that we actually did disagree. We've never been able to hold a conversation long enough for me to find out. We start, but before long we end up arguing. So I'm only guessing about whether we disagree or not. And suddenly, it seems important to find out."

Question 3:	Answer:	Distracting Thoughts and Worries:
Why do I want to work things out? • Focus on positive feelings and/or practical reasons.	If we could be calmer together, have the same rules for the kids, agree about who's to discipline them and how to do that, then I'd be able to stay married to him. I would like Michael and I to work things out and live like a loving family; it would be good for Sarah too.	If it weren't for Sarah, I'd give this more time. But I can't. It's not good for her to live like this, and I have to think of her first.

"Answering this question is like giving yourself permission to indulge in a bunch of wishful thinking about how nice it would be if we didn't have this problem. But real life is not that simple. I don't think our married life will turn out this way or even come close.

"When I finished my answer, I felt sad that there are good reasons to work things out and sadder that it's not likely to happen for Michael and me."

Question 4:	Answer:	Distracting Thoughts and Worries:
How would I like things between us to be? • Turn what you **don't** want into what you **do** want.	I'd like us to be calm around the kids and enjoy each other like we used to. I'd like us to be polite to each other and the children. ~~Instead of reacting every time they do something that one of us doesn't like,~~ I'd like us to agree on how to deal with Sarah and Ben. I'd like Michael to do many things differently. ~~Specifically, if he thinks Sarah eats too fast or watches shows~~	I'd like to go back in time, because things were better between us and the children when we were just dating.

Question 4: (cont.)	Answer:	Distracting Thoughts and Worries:
	~~he doesn't approve of, I want him to talk to me instead of picking on Sarah. He could say, "I feel worried when I see Sarah eat so fast. I don't think it's healthy. Are you concerned too?" or, "I'd like to talk to you about what TV shows Sarah watches. Some of them look violent. Could we see if we can agree on a list of shows that are appropriate for both kids and set some TV rules for them?~~ ~~And if we argue about rules for Sarah, I want Michael to say, "I don't agree with you, but I'll follow your lead with Sarah."~~	My answer is getting too complicated.
• What would the perfect partner do?	My perfect partner would help me figure out what our problems are and pick one problem at a time to deal with. I'd like Michael to be my "perfect partner in communications". That means	
• Specify your partner's realistic actions.	he'd sit down with me and listen to what I see as our problems. Then he'd pick one problem and say it's a problem for him too. Then he'd brainstorm with me about how we could solve that	

Question 4: (cont.)	Answer:	Distracting Thoughts and Worries:
	problem. And he'd agree to try the best solution we come up with. If it worked, we'd pick another problem to handle together. If it didn't, he'd agree to brainstorm some more or go with me to seek professional advice.	

"Because we have so many different problems, at first I had trouble answering this question. I went back to my answer to Question 2 *(What's the fairest way to describe the problem?)* and tried to address each of our problems separately.

"I think when I was reading all those other stories in this book, it seemed like people answered this question by writing down *exactly* what they wanted their partners to say. So I assumed that I'd have to figure out what I'd like Michael to say to me in order to settle each of our problems. I tried answering the question that way for about a page, and then I realized that if it was taking me this long to write out exactly what I wanted him to do, I'd never be able to get all my points across to Michael in person. So I crossed that stuff out. Then I started writing about how Michael could help me figure out what our problem was. I knew I wanted us to try to solve things together. So then I just wrote down how I'd like him to do that."

Question 5:	Answer:	Distracting Thoughts and Worries:
How can I actually get that? • Keep your goal in mind. • Handle worries. • When, where, under what circumstances?	I want Michael to be my "perfect partner in communications," so on Saturday night when Sarah leaves for an overnight with her scout troop and Ben's going to be at his mother's house, I can make a special	It's impossible to bring this up when the kids are around. I won't tell him my plan in advance because one time I did, and he got so worked up that I spent hours trying to

Question 5: (cont.)	Answer:	Distracting Thoughts and Worries:
	dinner for the two of us. I can use the quiet time after dinner to talk with Michael. To prepare, before Saturday, I'll try to think of every problem we have and write each one down on an index card. I'll probably end up with two dozen cards.	reassure him, and we never got around to talking about our relationship.
• Specify your actions.	Then I can toss the cards in a bowl, cover the top with foil, and put it on the table when I serve coffee and dessert.	
• Rehearse blame-free statement.	When he asks what it is, I'll tell him it's a recipe for a dish I like to call, "It's nobody's fault, but man, do we have problems". Then I'll smile sweetly and begin to read each card out loud. So this isn't a total downer, I'll make sure a few of the cards are humorous. And I'll keep my voice light as I read them. When I finish, I'll tell Michael I'd like him to pick one card that is also a problem for him and to brainstorm with me about how to solve the problem. And finally, when we have the best solution we can come up with, we can agree to try it and see if it solves the problem.	

"I am not a particularly clever problem solver. I'm more the serious kind of person who believes in talking about a problem until you have some idea about how to solve it. But when I read the stories in your book, I began to appreciate how important timing is and how important the way you bring things up can be. So that's probably why the idea for writing things on index cards—which came from one of the stories I read in this book—crept into my answer. But I'm not sure where the idea for putting one problem down on each card and calling it a 'recipe for all our problems' came from.

"Even though it seemed to me that Michael would be able to talk about our problems with me if I followed through with this "recipe for all our problems" idea, probably because it made things so concrete, when I reread what I'd written, my stomach sank. I have very little confidence that I could really do something like this."

Question 6:	Answer:	Distracting Thoughts and Worries:
And if that doesn't work, what else can I do?	If Michael won't go along with my "recipe for our problems" idea, or if we try it and it	
• When, where, under what circumstances?	doesn't work, then right away I will ask him again to come	
• Specify your actions.	to a therapist with me. I will	
• Rehearse blame-free statement.	tell him that the problems we have are no one's fault but that we have so many that I want him to pick one problem	
• Keep your goal in mind.	we can start to work on and that a one-time visit with a professional could really help. And if he refuses because he	Michael is so damn dead-set against going for therapy because of what happened when he and
	has had a bad experience with going to a marriage	his ex-wife went that I
• Handle worries.	counselor in the past then all I can think of is to ask him to meet me for lunch one day	may never get him to do this.

Question 6: (cont.)	Answer:	Distracting Thoughts and Worries:
	next week, and then we will use our cell phones to call the **Dr. Joyce** show. She's a radio psychologist who gives pretty good advice. And we don't have to tell her our real names. I think I can get Michael to try this because it is so anonymous and because one time he mentioned that he liked something he had heard her say on her program.	

Outcome

"On Saturday night, I went ahead and did what I said I'd do in my answer to Question 5. You know how I said that I wanted Michael to be 'the perfect partner in communication'? Well, I thought that meant that Michael would just listen to *me*. I forgot that I would need to be able to listen to *him* too.

"Michael listened to me read all the way through the cards. But when it came time for him to pick one problem for us to work on solving, after he picked a card, he started rambling all over the place. I swear it sounded as if Michael were trying to answer all six of the basic questions at once.

"In order to be able to follow what he was saying, I found myself asking him some of your questions out loud. Like, '"How would you like things between us to be?"' and, '"How can we actually get that?"' And his answers really helped both of us communicate better. We ended up knowing what we wanted as individuals and as a couple, and we even had a pretty good plan to deal with Ben's labeling of me as his 'evil stepmother' and Sarah's tendency to practically inhale her food!

"None of this probably strikes you as an earth-shattering conclusion, but it is to me. Before now, we haven't been able to talk about a single issue without one or both of us ending up disappointed or hurt. This time however, the 'evil stepmother' and her husband have a plan. And whether it works or not, we've agreed to keep trying."

Observations

Joan found that she could use her answers to the basic questions to think about each of her problems separately. One of the most helpful things she discovered showed up in the comments she made as she reread her answer to Question 2 (*What's the fairest way to describe the problem?*): "So, I'm only guessing about whether we disagree or not. And suddenly, it seems important to find out."

With that realization, Joan turned her attention to planning ways to communicate directly and effectively with her husband. Ultimately, she enrolled him in helping her decide which problem they should tackle first. Any time you are able to involve your partner in choosing the specific problem the two of you will address, it is much more likely that both of you will hang in there and keep trying even if (or when) things get tough.

A Perfect Mess

When Stan, a never-before-married man in his early thirties, married Rachel, a widow with a four-year-old daughter named Jennifer—he was thrilled to become an instant dad. And he looked forward to having more children in the future. However, Stan soon discovered that his way of parenting was so much at odds with his wife's that their relationship was beginning to erode. His story is a wonderful example of how the basic questions can help you move forward together even when you can't get your spouse to see things from your point of view. Here is what Stan said:

"Rachel and I always said we wanted two or three kids. So last night, when I brought up the topic of having another child, I thought she'd be pleased, but she told me she's too unhappy about the way I deal with Jennifer and the normal mess that kids her age make to have another kid. I didn't even realize this was such a big deal until she said that. It's true that I think Rachel is too soft on Jennifer and she thinks I am too hard on her. But does that mean we can't have more kids?

"Jennifer's always making a mess. Toys everywhere. Toilet paper pulled out and carried all the way down the hall. Food dropped all over the place. But try to do something about any of this and Rachel gets all huffy.

"Just the other day, she said, 'I think you were too hard on Jennifer when you yelled at her for dropping her ice-cream cone in the car.' And I said, 'Jennifer wasn't paying attention to what she was doing. How do you think she's going to learn? You're so soft on Jennifer; you're going to turn her into a spoiled mama's girl.' I guess you can tell that conversation didn't turn out too well."

Below you will see how Stan answered the basic questions. We would like you to notice how the coaching cue *What would the perfect partner do?* led him to what Stan calls, "a perfect solution to the whole mess!"

Question 1: What are my negative feelings?

Upset because now I find out that Rachel may not want to have another child. *Angry* at her for dropping this bomb on me without any warning. *Worried* about what to do now, and *anxious* to fix this quickly.

Question 2: What's the fairest way to describe the problem?

I want to have more kids. Rachel used to want that too. Now she's not sure. She thinks that I am too hard on Jennifer. I think she's too soft. We need to settle this before we have more children.

Question 3: Why do I want to work things out?

Because I want us to have another child, and I want to have less friction between us about how to raise our kids.

Question 4: How would I like things between us to be?

I would like us to resolve our differences about Jennifer immediately and to see if there is any room for compromise here. I'd also like to prevent our future disagreements about raising children from turning into the kind of stand-off we are in now.

(*What would the perfect partner do?*) The perfect partner would handle things directly, much as I do at work. First, as soon as she noticed there was a problem, she would schedule a convenient time to sit down with me. At that meeting, she would work with me to develop a long-range plan for raising our children. She would begin by asking me what I wanted to accomplish in the long-term and in the short-term, and she'd compare that to what she wants to accomplish. Then, together, we would hammer out a plan to blend our goals, define a shared objective, identify steps to get there, and build in periodic meetings to evaluate our progress and make adjustments as needed to keep heading in the right direction.

Question 5: How can I actually get that?

There's no way Rachel's going to handle things in such a straightforward, businesslike way! I can't imagine getting her to do things the way the "perfect partner" would. I'm stuck. (*Brainstorm if you're stuck.*) The advice I would give someone else facing this problem is: Don't sit around waiting for the other person to do things the way you'd like them done. Start the ball rolling. Act like the perfect partner yourself, and (*When, where, under what circumstances?*) tonight after Jennifer goes to bed, ask Rachel to help develop a long-range plan for raising our children. Start by asking what she wants to accomplish in the long-term and in the short-term. Compare her answer to mine. Look for places of agreement. Then, hammer out a plan that blends our goals and come up with a shared objective. Talk about what steps we can take to get there and plan to meet at least once a week to evaluate our progress and make adjustments as needed.

Question 6: And if that doesn't work, what else can I do?

Give in and do things Rachel's way. (*Keep your goal in mind.*) At least then we could have more children.

Outcome

Five weeks later, Stan told us, "After Jennifer went to sleep that night, Rachel and I sat down and started to talk about our long-range hopes and plans for Jennifer. That went pretty well; we wholeheartedly agreed on the kind of adult we hope Jennifer will be. We saw that we agree on what we want Jennifer to learn from us, but we disagree on the best way to teach her those things. And when we got to that, we went right back to arguing about how to handle the day-in–day-out things like discipline.

"Out of desperation (because I didn't want to leave things like that) I said to Rachel, 'How about this? What if we both write down ten things that the perfect partner would do in this situation? Then let's see if we like any of the ideas either of us comes up with enough to end this evening with a hug and a promise to talk about it again tomorrow night.' The 'What would the perfect partner do?' part of Question 4 helped us to end that first talk with a hug, but nothing got settled.

"Since then, we've talked off and on about how different we are when it comes to raising Jennifer, but we aren't fighting about it—just listening. I asked Rachel to show me how she handles Jennifer's messiness. As I watched, I asked a lot of questions, and Rachel seemed pleased that I was doing that.

"Lately, when I look uncomfortable about the mess of living with a four year old, Rachel starts teasing me about trying to turn Jennifer into a 'good little soldier' and the way she does that makes me smile. So I guess you could say that Rachel and I are gentler with each other when we come up against our different ways of child rearing. More and more often now, I enjoy playing with my perfect little daughter as she makes a perfect mess of things. And I'm hopeful that there will be more kids in our future."

Observations

Before he asked himself the six questions, Stan was intent on changing his stepdaughter's messiness and on getting his wife to follow suit. Ironically, when he implemented his own plan of action, it was Stan who changed. We thought Stan's use of the coaching cue *What would the perfect partner do?* was especially effective and creative. If you find that you disagree about how strict and/or permissive to be with your children, it may be a good idea to have the kind of ongoing discussion that Stan initiated with his wife and to add in a dose of good humor along the way.

THOUGHTS TO TAKE WITH YOU

When you want to make your way past the pressures and pitfalls of life in a blended family, you may find it helpful to:

- Use the basic questions to identify, sort, and prioritize the problems you face.
- Read the stories in this book to find ideas and solutions you can try.
- Consider adopting the same problem-solving strategies that work for you in other areas of your life.

12

Oh My God versus
Oh Your God

Coping with religious differences

Is it realistic to think that interfaith couples can nurture and accommodate one another's spiritual lives? What if the external symbols of one partner's faith rankle or upset the other? Can spouses overcome disputes that arise from their separate traditions about the rights and responsibilities of their children?

When a couple's religious beliefs, customs, and holidays are very different (and especially if they have children together) it's likely that the partners will butt heads over where, when, how, or even whether to worship. When individual notions of faith clash, one or both people can experience such strong negative emotional reactions that the possibility of a compromise isn't even an option.

In this chapter, you will hear from three individuals (two women and one man) whose partners are of different faiths. Their stories show how the six questions can help interfaith couples accept their partner's faith or lack of it without judgment and expand their awareness of their religious differences without feeling the need to agree.

None of their solutions is ideal. In fact, all are a little bit messy—as messy as real life generally is. However, each account illustrates something about the power of religious beliefs to separate us and the power of these very same beliefs to unite us.

Bigger Than a Christmas Tree

The story below is a good example of how the six questions can help people so clearly understand what they really want or need from their partners that an unresolvable conflict turns into a resolvable one.

Danielle and Henry have been married for four years. They have an eleven-month-old daughter whom they named Leanne. Henry is an observant Jew. Danielle is a lapsed Presbyterian who grew up in a nonobservant home. Before they married, Henry asked Danielle to raise their future children as Jews. She said she found it easy to say "yes". Danielle explains, "It just made sense to me that we would want to give our future children the same religious beliefs and traditions that held such deep meaning for Henry."

Recently, in the warm and happy spirit of her growing family and her fond memories from childhood, Danielle brought home a small Christmas tree in honor of Leanne's first holiday season on earth. She planned to ask Henry to help her decorate it that night. She didn't anticipate Henry's angry demand that she, "Get rid of that tree, right now!"

As you read her account of the events that followed, we want you to notice how, by tracking her personal answers to the six questions, Danielle learned that what she wanted was actually quite different from what she'd been asking for. And you will also see how knowing what she really wanted helped Danielle more clearly communicate her desires to her partner.

This is Danielle's story:

"After the scene he made, I carried the tree outside, but I had no plans to drop the idea of making Danielle's first holidays on earth a special time. To me, it's wonderful seeing presents piled up beneath a fresh-smelling evergreen tree that's been decorated with strands of tinsel, popcorn strings, sparkling lights, and handmade ornaments. The next morning I tried explaining how I felt to Henry.

"I said, 'Look, over the last few years, I've been okay going to my parents' home for their Christmas celebration. And I appreciate your coming along too. But now that we have Leanne, I want us to create the same kind of experience in our own home. And that's why I want a Christmas tree. Because it's a wonderful connection to my favorite childhood memories, not a religious icon.'

"Henry listened for a few minutes; then he interrupted and said that the idea of the tree was out! He sounded so fierce; I just stared at him without speaking. Later, before he headed out to run some errands, he gave me a quick kiss, and when I didn't react, he said that if what I really wanted was to decorate our house then I should do it, 'in a non-Christmas way.'

"'You can string popcorn along the wooden banisters leading upstairs, and for sparkling lights you can buy a flashing electric 'Hanukiah' (special Hanukkah candle holder that is lighted each evening during the eight days of the festival of lights) from the synagogue gift shop. And if you really want to go all out,' he said, 'why not make some painted dreidels (traditional spinning-top holiday toys) and put them in every window in the house?'

"When he left, I couldn't shake the feeling that I should be happy with the suggestions Henry had made—only I wasn't. I realized he'd handed me a reasonable solution to the problem. It was a solution that sounded good, but it just wasn't satisfying."

As she sat down to answer the basic questions, Danielle was still confused:

Question 1:	Answer:	Distracting Thoughts and Worries:
What are my negative feelings? • Toward whom?	**Angry** at Henry because, ever since I agreed to keep a Jewish home, I've had to give up things and he hasn't. **Maddened** that I can't figure out why his logical suggestions leave me cold.	He acts like bringing a tree home means I want to turn Leanne and him into Christians.

Question 2:	Answer:	Distracting Thoughts and Worries:
What's the fairest way to describe the problem?	I want a Christmas tree. He doesn't. We have both been unsettled since I brought one home.	

Question 3:	Answer:	Distracting Thoughts and Worries:
Why do I want to work things out? • Focus on positive feelings and/or practical reasons.	So I can give my daughter (and our future kids) the same sort of happy family experiences and wonderful childhood memories that my parents gave to me.	I just want our family holidays to be as great as mine were when I was a kid.

Question 4:	Answer:	Distracting Thoughts and Worries:
How would I like things between us to be? • Specify your partner's realistic actions.	I'd like us to be together, happy, and excited at holiday time like my parents were (and still are). Specifically, I'd like Henry to string popcorn, cook a holiday meal, wrap gifts, make decorations with me, and tell holiday stories.	I don't need a tree to make the holidays good, but I do need him working with me to make them great and I'm afraid he won't do that.

Question 5:	Answer:	Distracting Thoughts and Worries:
How can I actually get that? • Specify your actions.	Tell Henry I'd like him to help me put together a holiday dinner by: 1. Inviting our families over for a holiday dinner of turkey and latkes (potato pancakes). 2. Decorating the house with strings of popcorn and chocolate coins (traditional children's treat at Hanukkah). 3. Wrapping presents.	I'll plan the event since he hasn't done this kind of thing before. Luckily, Henry makes great latkes, and he's a terrific storyteller.

Question 5: (cont.)	Answer:	Distracting Thoughts and Worries:
• Handle worries.	4. Cooking the meal. 5. Telling one of those Hanukkah stories he told me when I was first learning about Judaism.	What if I ask for this but Henry is still too uneasy about what he thinks my motives are to go along with me? Start smaller?

| Question 6:

And if that doesn't work, what else can I do?

• Handle worries. | Answer:

I don't think Henry will fuss once he realizes I didn't ask for a Christmas tree. But if he doesn't like this idea, next year I can knit stockings with dreidels on them for each of us to hang on the back of our chairs during Hanukkah. Then each year, Henry and I can put notes about wishes for others into everyone's stockings. They can keep the those notes their whole lives. | Distracting Thoughts and Worries:

Might need other ideas if I have to keep trying to get this straight. At least now I know I want the two of us to work together a lot more than I want to hang stockings or decorate a tree. |

Outcome

"Henry *finally* agreed to help me with Danielle's first Hanukkah party. But it took a long time to convince him. We argued until, almost by accident, I asked him something that left him smiling.

"I asked if he had any warm family holiday memories. Henry thought about it; then he nodded and laughed as he told me how every year he and his family always wore the same costumes (different sizes of course), during a holiday called Purim. And he talked about how his family celebrated the harvest each year by eating outdoors in an open-air lean-to–like structure called a Sukkoth.

"Right in the middle of telling me about another of his family's traditions, Henry broke off talking, stood up, put his arms around me, and said he suddenly understood what I wanted and why. And while he wasn't all that crazy about decorating our house with popcorn or wrapping presents, he said he would do those things and more to make sure I knew how much he loved me, our daughter, and my vision of family life.

"We still have a few days left before our Hanukkah dinner, so I can't say whether this is going to work out well or not. But I can tell you that by going through the questions, I learned to see our problem from a different perspective, and now, I am not stuck in my anger."

Observations

Writing and rereading your answers to the questions can help you settle your religious differences. In this case, rereading her written answers helped Danielle move past her anger about the unfairness of her situation. Originally she said, "I want a Christmas tree…it's a wonderful link to my favorite childhood memories, not a religious icon." But by the time she answered Question 3, her description of what she wanted was quite different, "Specifically, I'd like Henry to string popcorn, cook a holiday meal, wrap gifts, make decorations with me, and tell holiday stories."

Her changed position also is reflected by the distracting thoughts and worries she had while answering Questions 3 and 4, "I just want our holidays to be as great as when I was a kid and I don't need a tree to make the holidays good but I do need both of us working together to make them great."

With those words, Danielle indicated she'd begun to think about the meaning behind her dispute with Henry. And from there she recognized that she had many more options—options far beyond her earlier assertion that a Christmas tree was the answer to her problem.

Teach Thy Children Well

As we age and lose people we love, we begin to question our purpose in this world, and we reconsider our beliefs about an afterlife. That's when our religious differences can take on a greater degree of urgency. And that's when an old conflict can re-ignite.

In the story that follows, you will hear how one man moved ahead and began to solve a problem despite his wife's lack of cooperation. We especially want you to notice that while he took steps on his own to get what he needed, he did so in a way that left open the possibility that his wife might participate with him in the future.

Although Lainie was raised in an orthodox church, she'd long since ceased participating in the rituals of her faith. She hardly ever prayed, and when she did she said it was more like thinking out loud. Eddie, the only son of a Methodist minister, was a committed agnostic. For their own reasons, each had turned away from organized religion. When they married, the couple agreed that any future children they might have would respect all religions but would not affiliate with any one faith. Currently they have two daughters, ages seven and eight.

This is Eddie's story about the change of heart that shook up his marriage:

"My dad suffered a long, lingering illness. He passed away three months ago. The time I spent with Dad helped me know him better and to see how deeply comforting his faith was to him. As he shared his thoughts about dying with me, I felt the need for the comfort of faith as well.

"But when I told my wife I wanted to add religion back into our lives, she exploded and said, 'No. I thought we agreed that our spirituality had nothing to do with organized religion. And we agreed that if we ever had kids we wouldn't force religion on them.'

"I replied, 'That was then!' Not a good answer, I know, but I didn't know what else to say."

Searching for a better way to approach his wife, Eddie answered the questions as follows:

Question 1: What are my negative feelings?

Not guilt! I've made the right decision. *Remorse* about having to go back on my original agreement. *Regret* at having made such a deal in the first place. *Uneasy* about getting Lainie to go along with me. *Unwilling* to let it go because it seems so important to have religion in our lives.

Question 2: What's the fairest way to describe the problem?

We began our marriage at a time when we were both turned off by organized religion. I don't feel that way now. Lainie does. I want to bring religion into our family life. She doesn't.

Question 3: Why do I want to work things out?

My decision about going back to praying in a church just feels good, and I believe it would be good for my wife and children too.

Question 4: How would I like things between us to be?

I'd like Lainie to get over her anger and agree that we can go to church as a family.

Question 5: How can I actually get that?

To move Lainie past her anger at me and get her to be receptive to coming to church, I can tell her some things my father said that really hit home with me. Like how Lainie and I had the freedom to stay or to walk away from the church. But our kids don't. By not exposing them to any formal faith, we've taken the right to decide that question out of their hands. We made that decision for them.

Then if she seems to be thinking about what I've said, I can ask her to keep an open mind and come with me to see if there's a church out there that might be a good fit for us. Maybe I can make this into a family adventure.

Question 6: And if that doesn't work, what else can I do?

Give it time. Meanwhile, explore churches on my own and find a way to share my experiences without pressuring her or the kids. Maybe over dinner with Lainie and the girls I can tell them what I have been learning at different kinds of churches.

Outcome

"When I finished the questions, I wasn't exactly awed by your problem-solving method. And I was unimpressed with how unstructured both of my action plans ended up being. But without any other ideas, I went home and tried to follow my answer to Question 5 (*How can I actually get that?*).

"At first, I talked to Lainie about what I'd felt and thought during the last months with my father. It didn't work. When I finished, she shook her head 'no' and said, 'I can't believe you! I'm not going to start making my kids go to church. You know how I felt as a child when religion was forced on me.'

"So I went to my back-up plan, as vague as it was. I visited churches and met people at each one. I wanted to share my experiences with my wife and daughters. So over dinner, I got in the habit of retelling parts of sermons I'd heard and sharing some stories about the quirky congregants I'd met.

"After a while, Lainie and the girls were clearly enjoying my reports. A few weeks into this, the girls asked if they could go with me the next time I went to church. I hesitated, but Lainie smiled and said, 'yes.'

"Then the girls asked, 'Mommy, will you come too?'

"Lainie told them, 'Not this time—maybe someday.'

"'Why not this time?' our youngest demanded.

"'Because when I was young, I *had* to go and I didn't like it,' Lainie replied.

"Our older daughter asked, 'Was your church like the ones Daddy goes to?'

"Lainie looked up at me and then she said, 'No, I don't think so.'"

Observations

What we liked most about Eddie's story was how consistently he aligned his actions with his written goal, "I would like Lainie to get over her anger" and "be receptive to coming to church."

Although he said he, "was unimpressed with" both of his action plans, it seems to us he built into his plans a particularly effective strategy, which was to encourage his wife to keep an open mind by creating a pressure-free opportunity for her to do that.

Eddie summed things up pretty well when he told us:

"When Lainie was young, a very harsh, almost punishing form of worship was forced upon her. So I knew that proselytizing was not going to work. But I thought that giving her time and space without pushing it might. Even though we're still in the talking stages, it's starting to look like Lainie is willing to rethink things, so I'm feeling encouraged about her and about the helpfulness of your six questions."

In Good Faith

When we are young and in love, it's hard for most of us to imagine the impact that our different religious backgrounds and beliefs may have on our ability to succeed as a couple. In this story, a couple in the happiness of new love promised each other that they would raise their future children as members of both faiths. The trouble is that what seemed like a fine idea in advance began to feel very different as their children grew.

That's the dilemma that Annette, a deeply religious Jewish woman; her husband, Allen, a devout Roman Catholic; and their two sons, ages eight and eleven, faced.

Annette describes her situation this way:

"We were married in a beautiful ceremony by both a rabbi and a priest. All of our guests were stunned at how many prayers are identical in both liturgies. But our faiths are not identical enough to keep conflicts from popping up.

"We had decided we'd bring up our future children in both faiths. I was afraid it would be too complicated. But for the past eleven years (since the kids came along) things have rolled along smoothly.

"However, we are at that time when our oldest son, Sean, is supposed to start studying for his Bar Mitzvah, a coming-of-age ceremony usually celebrated during the child's thirteenth year. Sean's Hebrew studies are really important to me. I want to make certain that if, later on, he chooses to become a practicing Jew, he will have had the necessary training and education to do so with comfort and conviction. But I ran into trouble when Sean found out he had to attend Hebrew classes three times a week between now and his Bar Mitzvah.

"A couple of weeks ago, he refused to go to Hebrew school because he wanted to play baseball. I said he had to go, but Allen said if Sean wanted to play baseball instead of going to Hebrew school three times a week—that he should be able to make up his own mind.

"I said that was ridiculous. 'Any eleven-year-old would choose to spend his time playing with his friends instead of pursuing his religious studies. And why aren't you backing me up like you should? For all these years I've kept *my* part of the bargain. We celebrate Christmas with your family and Easter too. I even co-chair our neighborhood's annual Easter egg hunt. And now what happens? You pull the carpet out from under me!'"

Below are Annette's answers to the basic questions. Some of the distracting thoughts that cropped up for her along the way are included in parenthesis:

Question 1: What are my negative feelings?
Angry that Allen didn't keep his promise and I did. *Distrustful* of him. *Determined* our sons will be Bar Mitzvahed. (If the boys choose not to be Jewish in the future, it will hurt, but I'll try not to let that show.)

Question 2: What's the fairest way to describe the problem?
We agreed to raise our children in both faiths. I kept my part of the bargain, but Allen didn't. We've been arguing about this for weeks. I want to straighten this out.

Question 3: Why do I want to work things out?
So I can trust my husband to keep both faiths alive in our family.

Question 4: How would I like things between us to be?
I would like Allen to honor his promise that we'd raise the kids in both faiths. And I'd like him to do something so these kinds of arguments won't happen again.

Specifically, I want him to sit down with Sean and me and to say, "Your mother and I have decided that you will go to Hebrew school because we want you to be Bar Mitzvahed." (But what if Sean balks and says something like, 'That's not fair, Dad. You didn't have to be Bar Mitzvahed?') And if Sean balks, I want Allen to say, "Sean, so that I can play a role in your Bar Mitzvah ceremony, I will come and sit with you through one of your classes each week."

Question 5: How can I actually get that?
I wish that before we got married I'd thought to ask the rabbi and priest who married us how we're supposed to pull off this dual-faith thing. Maybe we could

meet with them now. If they're still around, I can find their phone numbers. And I can probably get Allen to go with me because he liked both men a lot. I'll call this week and try to make an appointment.

Question 6: And if that doesn't work, what else can I do?

If for some reason Allen won't do this, I'll meet with the rabbi and priest by myself and get their advice on how to raise children in one household with two faiths.

Outcome

"It only took me four days to locate both religious leaders. I made an appointment for us with each of them. Allen was fine about coming to both meetings—I had thought that would be the case. I figured he'd be anxious to do something to get himself out of the dog house with me.

"We met with the rabbi first. He listened to both of us say what the problem was and then he said a lot of the things you'd expect a learned and kind man like him to say. Then he turned to Allen and explained that fathers play a special, almost elevated role in the lives of their sons—and that because of that, it was going to be especially meaningful for Sean if his father would involve himself in pre-Bar Mitzvah studies at least six months before of the event.

"Then he picked up the phone and called our rabbi. Before he hung up, he arranged it so that during baseball season, Sean would only have to go to Hebrew school on Saturday mornings. He said Sean could do the rest of the work at home and bring it to class with him on Saturdays. When we left, I was happy knowing Allen would play a big part in Sean's Bar Mitzvah. And Allen was happy knowing that Sean would be able to remain on the baseball team with his friends.

"So, we both felt as though we'd gotten our way.

"Then we met with the priest, who said he was proud of us for asking difficult questions and for seeking advice from leaders of both faiths. He told us that nowadays there are many more premarital classes available to interfaith couples than when we got married. He suggested it might be a good idea if we looked into attending one of those.

"He gave us a brochure with some course descriptions and class schedules. He also encouraged us to take continuing-education classes together. At least two courses each year would be ideal, he said—one about Catholicism and the other about Judaism. I think we might do that. Allen likes classes where you don't have to pass exams or write papers, and so do I. On that we definitely agree."

Observations

Writing out her answers to the six questions gave Annette a structured way to come to grips with the conflicts that were built into their decision to raise a family in both faiths. The wording of the questions seems to have prompted her to come up with a plan in which the two of them would seek advice from trusted religious leaders ("…ask the rabbi and the priest how we're supposed to pull off this dual faith thing").

In this case, their short-term problem of baseball versus Hebrew school for Sean was worked out with help from the rabbi. The priest addressed the long-term challenge of raising a dual-faith family by suggesting that together, they immerse themselves in an ongoing education about both religions.

THOUGHTS TO TAKE WITH YOU

When coping with religious differences, it may be helpful for you to:
- Reread your written answers all along the way.
- Align your actions with your written goal.
- Seek advice from trusted religious leaders.

13

Sick of Sickness

When serious health problems strike

If you or your partner becomes gravely ill or if one of you suffers a serious injury, it's normal to feel swamped by a host of negative emotions like anger, anxiety, guilt, and hopelessness. Unfortunately, it's seldom easy to discuss those feelings with your partner. But holding back can put so much more emotional distance between the two of you that it's likely to make things worse. So what can you do?

Here, you will watch four people grappling with a variety of serious health problems (breast cancer, paralysis, mental illness, and terminal disease) ask and answer the six questions in order to begin to talk about and work through their resentments, confusions, and worries. And you'll see that doing so fuels each person's desire to reconnect with his/her partner from a position of honesty, love, and trust.

None of these people awoke one morning having suddenly reestablished a deep connection with their partners. It doesn't happen that way. Reconnecting happens slowly in spurts and baby steps until the day comes when you realize that you're able to express your genuine emotions and concerns with your partner; understand and accept your partner's way of dealing with illness; and adapt to the changes that living with serious, chronic, or life-threatening health problems necessitates.

Everything Is *Not* Fine!

The problem-solving model presented in this book can be especially helpful to people under great stress—including those who no longer see any light at the end of the tunnel. This straightforward, step-by-step, question-and-answer approach seems to provide them with a structured, methodical way to look at their problems again.

In this story, Deborah, a woman who'd recently learned she has breast cancer, is understandably upset and confused. She told us she doesn't know what she wants from her husband, Richard. All she knows is that she'd like him to stop acting as if everything is fine.

Deborah describes her situation below:

"Many years ago, my aunt and two of my cousins died from breast cancer. Then, six years ago, my youngest sister died from the same thing. Shortly after that, my older sister, Janice, found a lump in her breast. Now, after a long uphill battle, Janice's cancer seems to be in remission.

"In the past, I've gone with my sisters to dozens of doctors. So I know all about the latest treatments and the improving survival rates. But that doesn't make a damn bit of difference when your doctor turns to you and says, 'You have a malignancy.' I couldn't hear anything she said after that. I was screaming inside my head, and I guess I went into shock. I came to at the point where she was saying she'd already scheduled me for a double mastectomy and two or three months of radiation and chemo.

"The closer I get to my surgery, the more terrified I am. But when I start to tell Rich how I feel, I can't finish a single sentence before he jumps in and insists that everything's going to be fine.

"I know he means well, but the way he's acting doesn't help me. I don't know what I want from him, but that isn't it. I understand that I'm the only one who can battle with my cancer. But I feel so alone."

You'll find Deborah's written responses to the six questions below:

Question 1:	Answers:	Distracting Thoughts and Worries:
What are my negative feelings? • Pay attention to all your negative feelings.	**Alone. Terrified. Depressed. Worried** about my life, my body, my husband.	Will I look so ugly that Rich won't want to touch me?

Question 2:	Answers:	Distracting Thoughts and Worries:
What's the fairest way to describe the problem? • What do we usually do? • No blaming, explaining, or guessing.	I'm scared of what's to come. I try to tell Rich that, and he rushes in to say it's all going to be just fine. ~~He probably just wants to reassure me, but~~ when he does that, I feel even more alone.	Don't want to hear things will be fine when no one can know that.

Question 3:	Answers:	Distracting Thoughts and Worries:
Why do I want to work things out? • Focus on positive feelings and/or practical reasons.	This is going to get a lot worse before (if) it gets better, and it would help me to be able to say whatever I want to Rich ~~without him cutting me off to say everything will be fine when he can't possibly know that~~.	Time to get real.

Question 4:	Answers:	Distracting Thoughts and Worries:
How would I like things between us to be?	Before my surgery, I'd like us to be truthful with each other. I'd like Richard to really listen to me ~~without interrupting to say, "I'll be fine"~~ so I could tell	Rich doesn't discuss feelings. Not mine. Not his.

Question 4: (cont.)	Answers:	Distracting Thoughts and Worries:
• Specify your partner's realistic actions.	him about my fears and how deeply I love him. Then, I'd like him to just hug me and not let go until I do.	

Question 5:	Answers:	Distracting Thoughts and Worries:
How can I actually get that? • Keep your goal in mind. • When, where, under what circumstances? • Specify your actions. • Rehearse blame-free statement.	How can I get Richard to listen to me? His parents are bringing dinner over tonight, but they leave early. When they do, I can tell him I need to talk about something important and that I want him to let me finish before he says a word. And no matter what, I don't want to hear the words, "Everything is going to be fine." Then I'd say that until this whole cancer thing is over, in order for me to feel safe, I need to know I can tell him anything—even how terrified I am. And that I want to tell him about my loving feelings and my fears. And all he has to do is just listen, hold me in his arms, and let me cry.	He hates talks likes this. What if he can't handle this?

Question 6:	Answers:	Distracting Thoughts and Worries:
And if that doesn't work, what else can I do? • Specify your actions. • When, where, under what circumstances? • Keep your goal in mind. • Handle worries.	I'd like to keep this between the two of us, but after I ask, if he still can't listen to me say how scared I am or let me cry, I'll call Janice. I'll ask her to bring her husband with her and come over right away if she can, or if not, then the following evening. I'll ask them to stay in the room with Richard and me while I talk about what's going on inside me. That way, I'll get what needs to be said out in the open, and I can trust Janice to understand what I need and what Rich needs too, and she'll take it from there.	What if Janice can't come over?

Outcome

Deborah shared this with us before her surgery:

"I managed to get Rich to sit and listen to me. For the first few minutes he was pretty uneasy, but I kept on talking and he hung in there. I told him how much I needed him, that I understood how frightened of losing me he was, and that I was scared too. When the words, 'I am afraid I'll be so ugly after this that you won't want to make love to me anymore,' burst out of me, I started sobbing.

"Rich held me until I quieted, pushed my hair back off my face, and said, 'Sweetheart, it's you that I make love to, not your breasts.' Then, at last, we were talking about our feelings.

"Rich said that he had so much fear inside of him that every night after I'd taken my pills and gone to sleep, he'd been staying awake to check that I was still breathing. That touched me so deeply that I cried again, and Rich broke down too. Ever since then, when things get shaky, we've been able to comfort each other.

"I'm still terrified of what's to come. I still have to wage the fight of my life. But I don't feel as if I'm doing it all by myself anymore, and that helps."

Observations

Tracking her thoughts and feelings as she answered each question, Deborah was able to step out of the chaos surrounding her disease long enough to clear her head and look inside herself for ways to strengthen her connection to her husband. We think her story does a great job of showing you how the basic questions make it possible for people who are under enormous stress to take the kinds of small steps that can profoundly improve their experience.

Here's how Deborah explained it:

"I was so overwhelmed and my life was spinning so out of control that I could barely function. But with each question I answered, it got easier to shove my terror and worries off to the side so I could hear my own thoughts and make some decisions. I hadn't been able to do that since my diagnosis."

In this case, Deborah found she could tolerate the terror and uncertainty of her future once she knew she wasn't facing it alone in the present. She came through her surgery with flying colors, and her prognosis is very good. Answering the basic questions paid off for Deborah before the surgery by helping her share her fears and loving feelings with her husband in a way that let her feel heard and comforted. She tells us they have continued to communicate more honestly.

Film at Eleven

This story demonstrates that it really is possible to move forward together even when one person stubbornly refuses to cooperate. We've included it here especially for people whose marriages have been forever changed by one partner's physical limitations. However, we hope that it encourages everyone to let their personal answers to the basic questions lead them toward new ways to adapt to altered circumstances whenever life throws them a curve.

Here, Heather, a young married woman, shares what her life and marriage have been like since a skiing accident left her husband, Matt, paralyzed:

"Six years ago, Matt was healthier than me. He ran six miles a day, went hiking, mountain biking, played tennis, etc. Two years ago, a skiing accident changed all of that. Matt was twenty-nine, and I was twenty-seven when we learned he would have to spend the rest of his life in a wheelchair.

"Looking back, I wish I hadn't assumed there was plenty of time for me to have kids. Now it's too late. I feel sorry for myself sometimes. I envy strangers who look like they have a carefree life, and I resent married couples our age who are planning 'normal' futures.

"I work full time because we need the money. Insurance only pays part of what it costs to have a caretaker here every day. Matt needs someone to bathe and dress him and help him do ordinary things, like go to the bathroom. Along with cooking, cleaning, and paying the bills, I handle all the details of our lives, and I try to find things of interest to talk about with Matt.

"Once, I suggested watching the Olympics on TV, but he didn't respond. Then, at election time, I tried to get him to share his opinions about the candidates. Matt used to have lots to say about that, but again he didn't respond. The first and only time he showed any interest was when I used our computer to make a video tape of his friends wishing him well.

"Basically, Matt only speaks to me when he needs something done. And he's usually so short tempered that I have to clench my teeth to keep from snapping back at him. There's a lot of time when I think, 'Oh my God, is this what it will be like for the rest of my life?' About the only time we're calm around each other is when we watch the eleven o'clock news, which we do every evening."

Heather's answers to the questions follow:

Question 1: What are my negative feelings?
Sorry for both of us because we have no life. *Afraid* it'll always be like this. *Depressed* about not being able to have kids. *Angry* that he refuses to talk to me except to demand something. *Upset* for getting angry when this isn't anybody's fault.

Question 2: What's the fairest way to describe the problem?

I think our relationship is disappearing, and I don't want that to happen. I don't know what's going on in his head. He won't let me in. I am afraid to tell him what I'm doing or about my problems because compared to his, mine seem so trivial. So it ends up that we don't talk at all.

Question 3: Why do I want to work things out?

So we can try to make the best of things.

Question 4: How would I like things between us to be?

I'd like us to share a joke or be comfortable just sharing the same room and discuss how we feel. But to start with, specifically, I'd like Matt to talk with me about:

- how we see our lives in five, or ten, or twenty years;
- what we can do to make the best of things from this point on;
- how we can blow off steam without hurting each other's feelings;
- the pros and cons of alternative ways to have a child.

Question 5: How can I actually get that?

Since at least we watch the news together, I can use that time to try and get things moving. He liked that video tape I made for him…maybe make another one? But it'll take more than one tape.

I can make a series of sixty-second tapes and play them when the commercials come on during the news. I can make the first tape tomorrow before I go to work. Then I can think about it all day to make sure I still like this idea before I play the first tape for Matt.

The next tapes could cover all kinds of things. On one, I can present a typical day in the life of me (a speeded up version of what I do in a day going by so fast that it looks comical). At the end I'd say, "It's all in how you look at things."

Other tape ideas:

1. my hopes for us and some ideas about how to make things a little better;
2. things I need his advice on (Play "If I Only Had a Brain," from the *Wizard of Oz*, in the background?);

3. heroes I admire (Add a Christopher Reeve interview; end with a current picture of Matt and the words "My Superman" dropped into the picture.);
4. my wish to do something normal, like gossip (Start telling a really juicy tidbit and when I get to the best part say, "And now, back to the news.").

Question 6: And if that doesn't work, what else can I do?

I can be patient and make even more tapes. And I can keep playing them when the eleven o'clock news goes to commercials. I can make some of the messages clever or funny and others can be touching, and I'll make some of them really outrageous so he won't know what to expect. Hopefully, mixing it up like that will keep him interested enough to hear me out and get involved in some kind of conversation with me.

But if Matt starts to withdraw even further from me, then before he goes into the hospital next month for three days of testing, I'll locate a counselor who will see both of us while we are there.

Outcome

"Matt didn't react to my tapes for a while, but I kept making them anyway. His lack of response was disappointing, but making the tapes turned out to be fun for me.

"One day, about two weeks into this, I got off work earlier than usual. I went home and told the caretaker he could go ahead and leave. He sort of stammered around before saying he would rather stay since I was paying him for the next hour anyway. I thought that was odd, but I was glad to have some extra time to straighten the house and start dinner. When I was halfway finished, I heard the caretaker asking me to join Matt in the bedroom for a moment. When I got there, the room was dark, all the blinds were closed, and I heard Matt tell the caretaker to 'hit it and take off.' I was confused for a second, and then a video tape started up, and there was Matt, sitting in his wheelchair dressed in a suit and tie, saying, 'I would like to present to you, my viewing audience, a typical day in my life.' Then a speeded up version of his day came on the screen, and it ended with Matt saying, 'I guess it can be all in how you look at things.'

Observations

Heather's video tape idea struck us as wonderfully creative and entertaining. But we think there's another reason her messages connected with Matt despite his resistance. Rather than turn things into a heavy confrontation (which is what many of us tend to do), Heather kept it light; she kept it short, and she kept at it.

When what you need to say to your partner is going to be difficult for him or her to take in, conveying your needs with humor, determination, goodwill, and patience makes it more likely that your words will get through clearly and with impact.

Rising to the Occasion

In this account, Ron, a forty-one-year-old man, describes what it's like to be married to someone who became mentally ill. Brenda, his wife, lives at home but is often emotionally unavailable to him or their son, Justin. As you read, notice that asking the six questions helped Ron shift his attention away from something painfully difficult and unlikely to change and on to another area of his life where he could make a wonderful and positive difference. Here is what Ron said:

"Life with Brenda is no picnic. Her mental illness was diagnosed seven years ago, three years after our only child, Justin, was born. Brenda has had two suicide attempts since then. I love her, and I worry about her constantly. It's not easy to see her lying in bed, too depressed to get up or to be around when she's irritable and irrational at the same time, or watch her stay awake night after night or stop eating for days. It's a roller-coaster ride without the excitement.

"Although Brenda's illness takes up most of my free time, I'm concerned about Justin. When he gets home from school, unless it's one of those rare days when Brenda's more like her old self, her moods are so unpredictable that Justin tries to stay out of her way. He is spending more and more time closed up in his room.

"I know how he feels. Being with Brenda is upsetting and confusing for me too. She often has trouble thinking clearly. And if she gets focused on something, she just goes on and on about it until I can't take it anymore and I storm out of the room. Times like that, I feel like the lowest form of a man.

"So many things are screwed up for us now. I don't know if any of this can be fixed. Hell, I don't even know which way to go to try and fix things."

Take a look below to see where Ron's answers led him:

Question 1:	Answer:	Distracting Thoughts and Worries:
What are my negative feelings?	**Uneasy** never knowing what she'll be like when I get home. **Angry** that her illness has taken over our lives. **Frustrated** when I can't get through to her. **Worried** she'll try to kill herself again. **Worn out. Losing hope** she'll ever be stabilized or helped by her treatment. **Concerned** about Justin too. **Unsure** how to help him.	Justin deserves better.

Question 2:	Answer:	Distracting Thoughts and Worries:
What's the fairest way to describe the problem?	The only thing Brenda and I talk about now is how she's feeling. It's been a long time since we discussed how to be good parents. I'm worried that Justin's falling by the wayside.	Have to focus on what Justin needs.

Question 3:	Answer:	Distracting Thoughts and Worries:
Why do I want to work things out?	So we can raise Justin in as normal a way as possible. Plus, it would make me happy to do something good for our son, and it might help Brenda too.	Maybe we need a time when all three of us scream at the disease together?

Question 4:	Answer:	Distracting Thoughts and Worries:
How would I like things between us to be?	I'd like Brenda to be as involved with me as she can be in making decisions about raising Justin. I'd like us to sit down together and tell him that her disease upsets us too, that it's no one's fault, and that it's okay to be mad at how unfair this is.	

Question 5:	Answer:	Distracting Thoughts and Worries:
How can I actually get that?	I can do the following: **Plan** exactly what I want to say to Brenda so I'll be prepared to talk to her on her next good day. **Get** the whole thing set up to happen during Justin's winter vacation, which starts this week. I have two weeks off as well. **Say** I need her help to talk with Justin, and ask that we do so ASAP.	And if Brenda can't handle this?

Question 6:	Answer:	Distracting Thoughts and Worries:
And if that doesn't work, what else can I do?	If I can't get through to her by the end of the week, I'll talk to him for both of us. But I'm still going to try involving her in his life whenever she has a good day.	

Outcome

Here's what Ron told us: "The next morning, before I could tell whether it was one of her good days or not, I started a conversation with her about Justin. And she pulled herself together in a way that surprised me. I think I underestimated Brenda's ability to rise to the occasion for her son. She held it together long enough for the three of us to have that talk. Justin opened up about how he was feeling. Some of what he said was sad and hard to hear. But it's out on the table now—and we'll deal with it.

"What ended up happening was that all of us rose to the occasion. That might not sound extraordinary and maybe it's not a great thing. But it was a good thing for my family."

Observations

In the process of dumping out his feelings (in answer to Question 1, *What are my negative feelings?*) Ron's concerns for Justin became uppermost in his mind. And as he continued on through the remaining questions, rather than remain focused on the problems he was having in his relationship with Brenda, his concerns about Justin prompted him to enlist her help with their son. By talking to Brenda about something other than how she was feeling, Ron created an opportunity for them to work together and address an issue that was important to them both.

Focusing on Justin rather than on Brenda's illness made it possible for this husband and wife to relate more effectively than they'd been able to in years.

Once in a Lifetime

It can be deeply painful to watch your loved one's health deteriorate and to know that no matter what you do, you are about to lose the dearest person in the world. Below, you will read how a woman named Ada used the basic questions to help her connect with Harold, her terminally ill husband, as he neared the end of his life:

"I'm my husband's primary caregiver as he struggles through the last stages of an untreatable cancer. To know that his death is close by and that a lot of our desires are going to remain unfulfilled is terribly sad. I can already feel him withdrawing from me. While he's still here, I need as much of him as he can give me, and I still want to give something back to him. I don't know how to get that across to Harold, and I don't have a lot of time left to find out."

Ada anxiously answered the six questions. Her responses follow:

Question 1:	Answer:	Distracting Thoughts and Worries:
What are my negative feelings?	What are my negative feelings as I watch Harold approach the end of his life? **Resigned. Sad. Uncertain** how to reach him at least once more. **Afraid** I'll run out of time before I do this.	

Question 2:	Answer:	Distracting Thoughts and Worries:
What's the fairest way to describe the problem?	What's the fairest way to describe my problem? He's withdrawing from me already, and I want him to stay with me until the end.	

Question 3:	Answer:	Distracting Thoughts and Worries:
Why do I want to work things out?	Why do I want the end of his life to be different for us than it seems to be right now? Because I love him and I want him to stay with me as long as he can.	

Question 4:	Answer:	Distracting Thoughts and Worries:
How would I like things between us to be?	How would I like these last days to be for us? I want him to give me something I can keep in my heart, and I want to give him something to keep too.	

Question 5:	Answer:	Distracting Thoughts and Worries:
How can I actually get that?	How can I actually get that? I can see if the hospice people know what other people have done in situations like this. Or I can ask him what he wants during these last days, and then try to give it to him.	

Question 6:	Answer:	Distracting Thoughts and Worries:
And if that doesn't work, what else can I do?	If hospice can't help me, and if Harold doesn't answer when I ask him what he'd like, what can I do? Read him my answers to Questions 3 and 4 so maybe he'll hear me ask him to stay here while he can and also tell him how much I love him.	

Outcome

"Watching Harold fade in and out of consciousness, I sat down to think this out. I saw him open his eyes for a moment, so I took a chance and began reading my answers out loud. He shut his eyes again, but I thought I saw the slightest bit of a smile, so I went on and said, 'Harold, I want to know if there is anything I can still give you. And then I want to give you that.'

"Softly, Harold asked for my assurance that I would be all right. I gave him that. He also said he wanted to say goodbye to the people he'd loved during his life. Most of them were long dead, but he began speaking to them as if they were here in the room with us, and I got to listen to him talking to his friends and family in such a loving and powerful way, expressing the very core of his feelings, that I learned even more about this man I loved.

"Harold died ten days later. When he'd asked for the chance to say goodbye to the people he'd loved, he got that. And I got something too—a once-in-a-lifetime way to know Harold even more fully than I had before. I cherish that."

Observations

Although we tend to forget to use such an obvious strategy as coming right out and asking our partners for what we want, it's often the best way to get to a satisfying outcome. Even in a case such as this one (where Harold was in and out of consciousness), by reading her answers to the basic questions aloud, Ada found this strategy to be effective.

We also noticed that Ada wrote down each question at the start of her answers. She explained, "I was in turmoil. I needed to do that to keep my mind clear." We thought this was worth passing along in case, you, too, find yourself so overcome with emotion that you have difficulty remembering the questions.

THOUGHTS TO TAKE WITH YOU

When serious health problems affect your relationship, it may help you to:

- Add humor, determination, goodwill, and patience to your requests.
- Come right out and ask for what you want.

14

Infidelity and Other Gut-Wrenchers

Reconnecting when you don't know which way to turn

In this chapter, you are going to hear from people who feel betrayed, hurt, angry, frightened, and, in some cases, vengeful. They are reeling from a variety of gut-wrenching experiences including an infidelity discovered and the unbearable death of a child.

These are people who don't know which way to turn. Their relationships are on the brink of collapse. They can neither forgive nor forget. And yet, these people are about to show you how they managed to step back from the edge and strengthen their marriages.

The solutions they have come up with are neither surprising nor extraordinary. What is extraordinary, however, is the fact that each of the people presented here managed to work through inordinately difficult times and come out on the other side with their marriages intact.

As you read their accounts, we hope you will notice that the basic questions give people a solid framework in which to sort their feelings, focus on what they need in the moment, and decide what they want in the long run. But more importantly, what we hope you will discover as you read the next four stories is this: while the basic questions cannot save your marriage, taking the time to ask and answer them can turn the idea of getting a divorce into your back-up plan—instead of your only plan.

Our So-Called Marriage
This is the account of one woman's struggle to repair her marriage in the wake

of her husband's infidelity. Gina, a woman in her late twenties who had been married for three years, shares her experience below:

"Three-and-a-half weeks ago my husband, Dan, suddenly confessed he'd had an affair. He said he had ended it, and he told me he wanted to continue with our marriage. I was stunned. He was crying, begging my forgiveness, calling himself an idiot, insisting that he loved me too much to lie any longer, and telling me that now he understood just how important our marriage really was.

"I looked at him like I'd never seen him before and screamed, 'Don't you dare talk to me about our so-called marriage!'

"Since then, I've been going through the motions of living but not feeling anything. At night I cry a lot, and when I sleep I have nightmares. A few days ago, I started making plans in my mind about getting a divorce. I picked the attorney I'd go to. I thought about how much money I'd need every month, where I'd live, things like that, right down to what I'd tell other people.

"I thought about calling my sister because I knew she'd give me a place to stay and she'd never, ever forgive that son of a bitch for hurting me! The thing is, I thought about calling her, but I didn't.

"I don't know what to do. I'm too angry, too hurt, and too scared to think. I need to make some decisions, but how do you do that when you can't trust yourself? I mean, look who I married. I honestly thought Dan was too honorable to ever do something like this. How naïve can you get?"

Gina—like others in this chapter who found themselves caught up in such emotionally charged, intense, and chaotic situations that they had trouble thinking clearly—answered the basic questions slowly over a period of time. In this case, several weeks passed between the time that Gina wrote out her answer to the first question and the time that she sat down to tackle the remaining five questions.

Below are Gina's answers and the coaching cues she found most helpful:

Question 1:	Answer:	Distracting Thoughts and Worries:
What are my negative feelings? • Eliminate **should/ shouldn't**. • Replace or remove blaming words.	**Dying inside, devastated** by what he did ~~and his disrespect for me and our marriage,~~ **betrayed, foolish** ~~since I should have seen this coming~~, **rejected, hurt, unloved, fragile, afraid** to trust, and **furious** at him ~~for ruining our marriage~~.	How could he do this? Damn him! How could he do this to me? What am I going to do now?

Question 2:	Answer:	Distracting Thoughts and Worries:
What's the fairest way to describe the problem? • No blaming, explaining, or guessing.	Dan told me he'd been unfaithful. He said that he has ended things with the other woman and that he still wants to be married to me. Dan wants me to forgive him. I don't think I can. I don't know if I can stay married to him. ~~If he thinks that confessing before I found out on my own makes me think I can trust him to tell me the truth, he's a jackass.~~	

Question 3:	Answer:	Distracting Thoughts and Worries:
Why do I want things to work out? • Focus on positive feelings and/or practical reasons.	I think I still love him. I don't want to be divorced.	What good is love without trust?

Question 4:	Answer:	Distracting Thoughts and Worries:
How would I like things between us to be? • Turn what you **don't** want into what you **do** want. • Specify your partner's realistic actions.	I would like us to have a marriage based on trust, loyalty, and love. ~~I don't want to go through life worried every minute of the day and night about what he's doing or feeling suspicious.~~ I'd like Dan to go into couples' counseling with me and to follow any suggestions the therapist has. When I feel uneasy about how he is spending his time, I want him to answer my questions thoroughly and without resentment. I want him to promise to never again meet with or accept any phone calls from the "other woman." If she calls, I want him to tell me.	What if I never get over the hurt? How can I ever trust him?

Question 5:	Answer:	Distracting Thoughts and Worries:
How can I actually get that? • When, where, under what circumstances? • Keep goal in mind. • Specify your actions.	This weekend, I can tell Dan that it may take me a long time but that I really want to be able to feel trust, loyalty, and love toward him again and that to start, I want us to: 1. Work with a therapist (I'll find one today). 2. Rededicate ourselves to our marriage on our anniversary by going back	 If therapy doesn't help—there's no need to go any further.

Question 5: (cont.)	Answer:	Distracting Thoughts and Worries:
• Rehearse blame-free statement. • Handle worries.	to where we got married, having another ceremony—maybe call it a rededication?—and retaking our vows—write new ones? I can also tell Dan the truth, which is that one of my goals is to stop blaming him and that I don't know how to do that yet but that I hope a therapist can help with this.	How can I sound like I'm not blaming him when I am?

Question 6:	Answer:	Distracting Thoughts and Worries:
And if that doesn't work, what else can I do? • Keep your goal in mind.	Get a divorce. Going through that would probably be awful. But after that I could find someone I can trust and love—it just won't be Dan.	Living with someone who's messing around is worse than getting a divorce.

Outcome

About a week after she had finished answering the questions, Gina told us:

"Before I answered the questions, I was so afraid that I'd never be able to forgive or forget Dan's betrayal, that it was just easiest to lick my wounds and not do anything. And besides, in the beginning, part of me wanted to hurt Dan. I wanted to make him worry about whether or not his affair might have cost him our marriage. I don't know whether it was because enough time had passed or if it was the questions themselves—but by the time I finished answering them, I was feeling as if I wanted to work on things with Dan *more* than I wanted to hurt him back.

"So when a friend mentioned a couples' therapy weekend that she'd heard good things about, I told Dan about it and he said maybe we ought to start with that. I said 'okay' and he took it from there. In the past, the mention of a therapy weekend would have freaked him out, so it was strange to me that he took the lead and signed us up. And I think that's when Dan's sincerity started to get through to me.

"The therapy weekend turned out to be a safe place for me to unload a lot of my anger and to ask those wretched, awful questions about why he had done this to me. During the weekend, I began to see my own role in some of our problems. It was difficult and painful to see that there were problems of communication and intimacy present long before the affair, but it helped us start making changes by seeing how things had been.

"I left there feeling more optimistic about our future. Dan said he did too. After that weekend, we enrolled in a series of follow-up sessions to help us build additional relationship skills.

"Have I forgiven my husband for the lies and betrayal? Not completely. The hurt goes very deep. There are times when it comes to the surface, and I try to deal with it a little at a time. I don't dwell on it; it would eat me alive. Hopefully, someday it will be all gone.

"Our anniversary is next month. We're going to have what I call a 'ceremony of renewal' on that day. It will be a lot like it was for us in the beginning, but instead of saying, 'I do,' we'll be able to affirm that 'we do.'"

Observations

As she asked and answered the basic questions, the intensity of Gina's negative feelings decreased ("...in the beginning anyway, part of me wanted to hurt Dan. I wanted to make him worry about whether or not his affair might have cost him our marriage.")

We believe that the passage of time in combination with her efforts to answer the questions led Gina to concentrate less on how to get out of her marriage ("...how much money I'd need every month—where I'd live, things like that") and more on how to get back in ("We enrolled in a series of follow-up sessions to help us build additional relationship skills").

We hope that if you ever find yourself in a situation similar to this one you will take all the time you need to consider your options, and we hope that you'll allow your own answers to the basic questions to help you find and begin moving in a positive direction.

What Do You Want from Me?

This is another story about the impact of infidelity on a marriage. In this account, the spouses blame each other for the failures of their marriage and, to make matters worse, the partner who has strayed refuses to go for marriage counseling.

Our purpose in sharing this with you here is twofold. First, we want to illustrate how the basic questions can move you beyond the desire to blame so that you can more calmly and productively decide how or even if you want to reconnect with your partner. And second, we want to show you that—even in circumstances where trust has been shattered—one person can successfully move both people forward even if the other one seems unwilling to do much to help.

Mark and Gail had been married for twelve years when Mark learned of his wife's infidelity. He confronted her that evening and Gail admitted to the affair. She didn't stop there, however. She went on to tell Mark that she'd gotten involved in the affair to help her cope with what she said was Mark's "neglect" of her. Then, according to Mark, Gail unleashed a laundry list of things she said he had done wrong over the years.

Outraged at the suggestion that his behavior had in any way led to his wife's infidelity, Mark told us, "I can't believe my wife actually blames me for what she did. What a bunch of crap! Gail chose to have an affair. I sure as hell didn't okay it. So far as I'm concerned, this is all her fault. And I am angry!

"Gail refuses to come with me to couples' counseling. She says she doesn't need counseling. She told me she knows exactly what this marriage needs and that I'm the one who doesn't know a thing about our marriage.

"Gail says that over the years I've been hurtful, that my lack of attention to her has been destructive to our marriage, and that my neglect has brought us to this point in our relationship. She says she's tired of being taken for granted by me, and she feels let down. Yeah? Well guess what? She can get in line behind me!

"I asked her to break things off with this man she's seeing. She said she would end her sexual relationship with him but not her friendship. She told me that I used to make her feel sexy and interesting and that I used to act as if what she thought really mattered. She said she used to feel like she was the most special person in my life, but not now. Then she said that she gets those things from this other guy, so she's not going to toss him out of her life unless I can show her that I *really* love and appreciate her.

"'How can you say you don't know I love you? I'm standing here saying it over and over again. Why isn't that enough? How else am I supposed to let you know I love and appreciate you? What do you want from me?' I screamed in frustration."

Three months after their blow-up, Mark said that he and Gail had not made any progress. In fact, he said they'd not been able to get beyond shouting and finger pointing. Mark wanted to save his marriage. He wanted Gail to know he loved and appreciated her, and he still wanted her to go with him to see a marriage counselor—but he realized they had to stop yelling at each other first. So he decided to answer the basic questions to see if that would help. As you read Mark's responses below, please keep in mind that he wrote them over the course of several weeks:

Question 1: What are my negative feelings?
Furious at Gail. *Pissed* that she's trying to blame me for what she did. *Angry* that she won't stop seeing this other guy completely. *Worried* our marriage won't survive this. *Angry* she won't come to marriage counseling with me. *Confused* about what to do.

Question 2: What's the fairest way to describe the problem?
It has been six weeks since I confronted Gail about her affair. We still blame each other for our problems and for the fact that she had an affair. We both say we want to save our marriage, but we disagree about how to do that. Gail wants me to figure out how to make her feel special. I want her to come with me to see a marriage counselor so we can talk about how to straighten things out. So far, we are at a standstill on this.

Question 3: Why do I want to work things out?

I've been in love with Gail since we were in high school. I don't want to lose her.

Question 4: How would I like things between us to be?

I would like us to stop blaming each other, and I would like us to start working together to get our marriage back on track. Specifically, I would like Gail to tell me how to win her back even though she says I have to figure it out myself. I'd also like us to start seeing a marriage counselor.

Question 5: How can I actually get that?

To get us both to stop blaming each other for what's happened, I guess I can be the one to stop first. I can watch what I say and catch myself before I say anything that sounds like I am blaming Gail. And, so that we can start working together on fixing things, I can take Gail at her word. She says she needs me to show her that I love and appreciate her. To figure out how to do that, I can watch "Dr. Phil," read *Men Are From Mars, Women Are From Venus*, and keep after her to go into counseling with me.

Question 6: And if that doesn't work, what else can I do?

Go into therapy by myself. Keep trying all the different ways I can think of to figure out what she wants, and give it to her. Even if I don't do it perfectly, maybe Gail will give me credit for the time and effort I'm putting into trying to show her that I appreciate her.

Outcome

About six months after Mark initially confronted his wife, he told us:

"I had high hopes at first that if I just watched enough relationship talk shows, read enough books about what women want, or did enough thoughtful things for Gail that things would work out. I really threw myself into that.

"The hardest part was that I knew she was still in touch with that other guy and it hurt. I got depressed. Finally, I followed my own advice and did the first thing I wrote down in my answer to Question 6, which was, 'Go into therapy by myself.'

"I started going once a week, and some time after that, I stopped trying to compete with the other guy. I stopped clutching at every new idea I could think of to win Gail back. I didn't give up hope, but I gave up making it the entire focus of my life.

"When Gail said she noticed a change in me, I braced myself—fully expecting her to say she was leaving me. Instead, she said she was surprised that I had stopped accusing her of ruining our marriage. Until then, I'm not sure I realized I had stopped blaming her for everything.

"Then she said she appreciated what I was doing by going into therapy and that if I still wanted her to, she'd come with me to see my therapist next week. I don't know how this will end—but at least now we are starting to get somewhere."

Observations

It seems to us that the most significant thing Mark did here was to stop blaming Gail, because getting to that point can be especially difficult when feelings run high and the urge to blame seems not only appropriate but overwhelming. We asked Mark how he managed to do that.

He told us, "It didn't happen automatically—that's for sure. But it got easier after I made up my mind to stop saying that this was her fault. Blaming her only made things worse because she'd just come right back at me with a zinger, and we'd end up both yelling but never hearing each other. I think maybe it got easier to stop thinking about how angry I was at her when I answered Question 3 (*Why do I want to work things out?*) and wrote that, 'I've been in love with Gail since we were in high school. I don't want to lose her.' You know, you start thinking about what it would be like without your wife, and then you really think about what's important. I decided she was important.

"After that, my answers were all about how I could win Gail back and how I could get her into couple's therapy with me. Concentrating on those things made it easier for me to do something other than just keep blaming her. This isn't to say I don't have moments when I blame her, because I do. But they're moments, not hours or days or weeks like they used to be."

This story makes the point that even when one or both partners feel betrayed, asking the basic questions can direct your thinking toward getting what you want in the long run. When you can concentrate on something other than your own emotional upheaval in the moment, the intensity of your feelings lessens, your thoughts calm, and your mind clears—all of which can make it easier for you to hang in there and look for steps you might be willing to take in order to begin repairing your relationship.

The Unbearable Loss of a Child

In loving relationships, couples listen, give encouragement, and comfort each other to help ease the stresses that build up in everyday life. But in grieving for a child, parents may find it hard to think about supporting each other because their own feelings are so overwhelming. That was the case for Gary and his wife, Joanne, whose only child, fifteen-year-old Jessica, was killed in an automobile accident a little less than a year ago.

Here is a condensed version of how Gary described the impact that the loss of their daughter had on his relationship with his wife:

"7:05 P.M. That was the time our daughter left our home for the last time. At 8:50 P.M. that evening, a police officer came to the door and said, 'Sir, I have some bad news…'

"I was too shocked to speak. I've never known such pain. And I will always know it now. A day will never again go by that I don't relive that announcement, feel that rush of disbelief, protest, and then endless sorrow.

"People tell me Jessica's in a better place now. I don't want her in a better place; I want her here. And everyone asks me, 'How is Joanne doing?' No one asks how I am doing. I lost my child, too. I still stare at every teenage girl with red hair. I still ache all day, every day.

"Immediately after Jessica's death, Joanne and I grieved together. But since then, we've gone about things in separate ways. At this point, Joanne seems like she's doing fine, and I'm barely making it through the day.

"I don't know how Joanne can go to a movie or go out to dinner with friends—especially friends who have children the same age as Jessica. I feel jealous that Joanne's acting like she's okay, and I resent her for it too. I really think what she's doing is wrong—it's dishonest to go back to living the way we did before Jessica died.

"Joanne tells me she's tired of my grieving. She says that she's had enough of me moping around and that I can either go mad, or bury it and go on. She made it clear that she's chosen to bury it.

"When friends invite us out, Joanne keeps asking me to go, but I can't, so she's started going without me. I know I can't stay in the past—that I have to move on—but I haven't been able to do that."

Gary's written responses to the questions follow:

Question 1:	Answer:	Distracting Thoughts and Worries:
What are my negative feelings?	**Annoyed** at Joanne because she acts like she's over the pain of losing Jess. **Annoyed** that I'm not handling things as well as she is. **Afraid** I never will.	One minute you're a parent. Then, suddenly, you're childless. Nobody understands.

Question 2:	Answer:	Distracting Thoughts and Worries:
What's the fairest way to describe the problem? • We are different.	We are different in how we are handling Jessica's death. Joanne wants me to stop "moping" around. I want her to stop acting like everything is fine. Communication between us is strained.	

Question 3:	Answer:	Distracting Thoughts and Worries:
Why do I want things to work out? • Focus on positive feelings and/or practical reasons.	At no other time in my life have I needed my wife more——and at no other time has she been less available.	

Question 4:	Answer:	Distracting Thoughts and Worries:
How would I like things between us to be? • Turn what you **don't** want into what you **do** want. • Specify your partner's realistic actions.	I'd like us to talk together about the good times we had with Jessica ~~without feeling the agony of our loss~~. I'd like Joanne to accept my choice to stay home ~~without judging me~~. Specifically, I would like her to watch old family video tapes of Jessica with me, share her memories and stories about Jessica with me, and tell me how she's able to get on with things so much more easily than me.	

Question 5:	Answer:	Distracting Thoughts and Worries:
How can I actually get that? • Keep your goal in mind. • When, where, under what circumstances? • Specify your actions. • Handle worries.	To do something positive together, I can create a remembrance day on the anniversary of her death, which is next week. I'll include both sets of grandparents because they have stories and memories of Jess, too. Make this a celebration of her life—not more agony about her death. Ask Joanne to help think of a special program we can put together to honor Jessica and the things she loved in life.	 I don't think she'll want to do this.

Question 6:	Answer:	Distracting Thoughts and Worries:
And if that doesn't work, what else can I do? • Keep your goal in mind. • Handle worries.	If she won't help, come up with a way to set up a lasting tribute to Jessica on my own. And then, over the years, encourage Joanne to get involved in whatever I come up with here.	Maybe the grandparents will have an idea even if Joanne won't help.

Outcome

Below, Gary describes what happened after he'd answered the basic questions:

"I finished writing out my answers and went home without having any real plan for how to talk to Joanne. I assumed that the best thing to do would be to talk to her about anything except Jessica. And from there I hoped I'd find an opening to ease into asking her to help me plan a memorial for Jess.

"When I got home, though, I heard Joanne whistling to herself in the kitchen. I went in to say hello to her and all of a sudden, I heard myself asking her something odd. 'What do you say when someone asks how many children you have? Do you say, "I had one child," or "None?"'

"Joanne seemed taken aback by my question, but she sat down and we started to talk. I think that may have been the first conversation we had where I spoke about the loss of Jessica in a matter-of-fact voice. I didn't choke up. I really wanted to know how Joanne handles things like that.

"It was surprising and comforting to find that we had both been dumbstruck when someone asked that question. And then we just kept on talking. We talked about what we do when our emotions overwhelm us unexpectedly. It was interesting to see that we handle things like that very differently.

"From there, one question led to another, and for the first time in a very long time, I felt that I was with someone I could talk to who really did know what losing a child means. After that, it was easy to bring up my idea of a lasting tribute to memorialize Jessica. Joanne isn't quite ready to deal with that—but she has a few ideas we can put into motion in another year or so.

"I think that since we are grieving at different rates and in different ways, we have to stretch a little further than we used to in order to connect. I'm trying to do that, and so is Joanne. We joined a support group to learn how.

"People say that parents who work through this painful time together find that their relationship has strengthened. I don't know about that. But I believe that trying to work through this with Joanne is the only way I'm going to end up with any kind of relationship with her. And that's something I want very much."

Observations

The fact that Gary was willing to ask and answer the basic questions indicated that he already was beginning to emerge from the active-grieving stage. Again, the passage of time was a critical factor in his ability to reconnect with Joanne.

Still, there is something about asking the six questions that can engage people's hearts and minds differently enough that it becomes easier to move forward. In this case, when he finished answering the basic questions, for the first time in over a year Gary found himself initiating a spontaneous conversation with his wife. That seemed to us to be the turning point for this couple. No longer were they talking only about their daughter's death; now they were also talking about their life together in the wake of their loss.

When we can let go of the judgments that separate us, it's generally easier to reach out to one another. That is what Gary discovered when he began to ask Joanne about her way of coping with the same issues and problems that he faced. Early on, Gary described Joanne's behavior with the words, "I resent her... I really think what she's doing is wrong." Now, compare that to what he said after he'd answered the questions: "It was interesting to see that we handle things like that very differently."

Finally, we were impressed with Gary's interest in celebrating his daughter's life and the tribute he and Joanne hoped to establish. Both of their ideas are powerful and helpful ways to preserve our finest memories and move beyond the more painful ones.

THOUGHTS TO TAKE WITH YOU

In the face of infidelity and other gut-wrenchers, it can be helpful to:

- Answer the basic questions slowly, over a period of time.
- Be the first one to stop blaming.
- Let your personal answers draw your attention away from your emotional upheaval and on toward a plan of action.
- Consider making the idea of getting a divorce your back-up plan instead of your only plan.

15

Divorce and Other Endings

Connecting with goodwill through
loss, divorce, and life after that

Both of us strongly support taking whatever steps you can to settle your disputes and preserve your marriage. Still, we recognize that a lot of marriages don't make it to the finish line. Sadly, when a relationship fails, many people find themselves so trapped in a swirl of intense negative feelings that they end up distrustful of others and doubting their own ability to find love and happiness in the future.

In this chapter, we set out to show you that it really doesn't have to be that way. Here we will look closely at how four people managed to move beyond a relationship's end, resolve lingering issues with a former spouse, and improve their own chances for happiness in the future. In some cases, these people fashioned an ongoing, positive connection with their former spouses. In other cases, they moved on separately but with considerably less upheaval than had been anticipated. And in all four instances, they found that applying their answers to the basic questions made it easier for them to get on with their lives.

In the first account, you will hear from a woman who is embroiled in a hostile divorce. She describes her efforts to fight for an equitable financial settlement from her husband and, at the same time, convince him to work with her to make sure their children retain their sense of family. The story after that comes from a husband whose wife is descending into the darkness of Alzheimer's disease. He lays out his struggle to cope with an ending that may go on for years. Another account deals with a woman's choice to move on without her gambling husband. And in the last story of this chapter, a widow shares her struggle to choose between her loyalty to her deceased husband and her fullest participation in life.

We hope the experiences of these four people make it clear to you that tracking one's answers to the basic questions can move a person beyond an unhappy ending and make it possible to forge respectful, cooperative beginnings with a former (or soon to be former) partner.

The Unwedding

We selected this story to make the point that a split between spouses doesn't have to mean a broken family. Sarah and Todd had been married for eighteen years when they decided to call it quits. Their difficulty in reaching an equitable settlement was hurting their teen daughters, Ellen and Wendy.

Here is how Sarah described the situation:

"Trying to hammer out a reasonable financial agreement with Todd has put us at each other's throats. It has gotten so bad that we argue whenever he comes back to the house to pick up something he needs, visit with the girls, or ask me a question.

"Last night, things got even worse. We started arguing about who gets what, and we were really going at it when our youngest daughter, fourteen-year-old Wendy, stormed into the kitchen and screamed, 'Stop it! Just stop it right now! You're ruining our family—both of you. Ellen told me this is what divorce does—it destroys people. I said that neither of you would let that happen, but now I see Ellen's right. I hate you *both* for doing this to our family. I hate you!'

"Wendy's words brought me up short. I can't stand the way our fighting is upsetting the girls. I know I need to negotiate this divorce better than I am, but I can't afford to stop fighting for the financial support the three of us are going to need.

"I wish I could just wake up six months from now when everything has been settled. I guess it's a little too late for me to use the six questions since I'm already getting a divorce."

We said, "Maybe it's not. Would you like to try and see what happens?"

Below, you will find Sarah's written answers:

Question 1:	Answer:	Distracting Thoughts and Worries:
What are my negative feelings? • Toward whom? • Get rid of negative labels. • Replace or remove blaming words.	**Angry** at Todd for the problems in our marriage and **angry** at him for making this divorce so difficult. ~~He's being a selfish jerk!~~ **Worried** about how our girls will handle things once the divorce is final. **Afraid** they'll blame me for breaking up the family ~~since Todd is filling their heads with his side of things~~.	

Question 2:	Answer:	Distracting Thoughts and Worries:
What's the fairest way to describe the problem? • What do we usually do?	We are arguing our way through this divorce, which is making things more difficult for the two of us and destroying the girls' sense of family. When we try to decide who gets what, we usually end up shouting and saying awful things to each other.	Wish the girls didn't have to hear us fight.

Question 3:	Answer:	Distracting Thoughts and Worries:
Why do I want things to work out? • Focus on positive feelings and/or practical reasons.	To minimize the harm our divorce inflicts on the girls and to make sure that after the divorce they'll feel like they still have a family.	There's no talking to him—everything is a fight.

Question 4:	Answer:	Distracting Thoughts and Worries:
How would I like things between us to be? • Specify your partner's realistic actions.	I'd like the two of us to work together to make sure Ellen and Wendy are as okay as they can be with what's happening. Specifically, I'd like Todd to agree to confine our property-settlement arguments to places other than the house. And I'd like him to sit down with the girls and me and figure out how we can be a family now and after our marriage is dissolved.	Todd probably won't do this when he realizes it's something I want.

Question 5:	Answer:	Distracting Thoughts and Worries:
How can I actually get that? • Specify your actions. • When, where, under what circumstances? • Rehearse blame-free statement.	Email Todd today to say that Wendy's outburst got my attention and I'm worried that we seem to be hurting the girls. I could say, "Since we're having trouble talking about the financial terms of our divorce, I'd like to talk with you only about what we can do to help Wendy and Ellen. Can we meet this week at the house and talk about how to decrease the impact on our girls? First, we could figure out what we can say to them that might help, and then we can ask them to join us in a	

Question 5: (cont.)	Answer:	Distracting Thoughts and Worries:
• Handle worries.	family discussion. Please email me and let me know if and when you could come over here.	What if he's too angry to talk without blasting me in front of the girls?

Question 6:	Answer:	Distracting Thoughts and Worries:
And if that doesn't work, what else can I do? • Specify your actions	I can try to talk to Ellen and Wendy on my own, and afterward I can email Todd to let him know what the girls said.	

Outcome

"A few hours after I emailed Todd, he emailed back saying he agreed that our girls were reason enough to get our act together, and he suggested we meet three days later. When we got together, we were actually able to stay focused on the girls and our concern for them. We decided to let the lawyers handle our legal and financial matters. And we agreed to do our best to keep our anger at each other from spilling over in front of the girls.

"After that, we asked Wendy and Ellen to come into the kitchen. Todd and I served up big bowls of ice cream. Then we sat down and said we wanted to have a family discussion about how to get through the divorce without hurting them any more than we already had.

"Ellen said she and Wendy had seen something on TV about an 'unwedding ceremony' where the husband and wife formally took off their wedding rings and vowed to give each other their best wishes for the future. Wendy said she remembered that the divorcing couple promised to recall the good things they shared, to let go of any bitterness they'd felt, and to be gracious to each other in the future.

"At first, Todd and I laughed at the idea of doing something like that. However, the girls were quite serious, and eventually we said we would have that ceremony on the Fourth of July. We knew that by then we'd be legally divorced, and I think we liked the significance of getting unmarried on Independence Day.

"On July 4, the girls invited some of our friends and relatives to watch as we formally agreed to unmarry each other. Todd and I stood up and proclaimed that we were joined forever by our love for Ellen and Wendy. We promised to be there for our daughters now and in the future. Then just like we did at our wedding, we asked those present to support us in our new relationship."

Observations

Wendy's outburst was a quite a wake-up call for Sarah. It prompted her to use the basic questions as a way of focusing on keeping her anger at Todd in check and looking for concrete ways to enroll him in helping her protect Ellen and Wendy from some of the more hurtful consequences of their divorce.

We really liked Sarah and Todd's unwedding ceremony. It struck us as an innovative way for them to remain mindful about what mattered most to them—their daughters. And even more remarkably, it moved the two of them to do something they hadn't been able to do in years—pull together.

To Have and Hold On To

Arthur is in his sixties. He's been married to Charlotte for forty-five years. They have three adult children and five grandchildren. When Arthur learned that his wife was in the early stages of Alzheimer's disease, he shut down so completely that the only thing he remembers the doctor saying was, "Over the next five years, your wife will get progressively worse. I hope you will both use the next weeks, months, and years to prepare for the challenge ahead."

Here is what Arthur told us at the time:

"Charlotte took her diagnosis as an urgent call to tie up loose ends and she wants me to help her say farewell to family and friends. I've been doing that, but it is depressing to hear her tell people that she wants to say good-bye while she still knows who they are. I'm just dragging myself through each day.

"I want to keep my wife safe. I want her to be able to draw strength from the life we've built. It's alarming to know that in a few years Charlotte will be physically present but emotionally absent. The wife I know and love will be replaced by a person who doesn't even notice whether I am there or not."

To help him shift out of his despair and find ways to get moving again, we gave Arthur a copy of the six questions.

Here is how he answered them:

Question 1: What are my negative feelings?

Depressed about the future. *Angry* at the unfairness of this. *Dreading* what it will be like when she doesn't even know who I am.

Question 2: What's the fairest way to describe the problem?

Charlotte has Alzheimer's disease. I promised to be there for her 'in sickness and in health,' and I will be. I can handle the physical caretaking, but I don't know how I'll handle it emotionally when she doesn't know who I am anymore.

Question 3: Why do I want to work things out?

Soon, all I will have left will be the memory of her, and I want to make sure I hold on to that and to ~~not let my reaction to the shell she will become destroy~~ our love.

Question 4: How would I like things between us to be?

I would like to always feel kind and tender toward Charlotte. I would like to be able to be her caretaker with patience, humor, and gentleness when her disease takes over and she's not really here. Specifically, I'd like Charlotte to participate with me in having as many positive experiences together as we still can. And I would like to hear some of her thoughts and feelings about me *now* so that I'll have something to hold on to that's about us.

Question 5: How can I actually get that?

Since I'm already helping her say good-bye to people, I can start taping her visits with them. I can also set up the camera when the two of us are alone. Then, I can steer the conversation toward how we feel about each other and what we liked best about the things we've done together. And I can tell her I love her and record her response. I can start this project tomorrow when the kids come over.

Question 6: And if that doesn't work, what else can I do?

If the taping makes Charlotte uncomfortable, my second-best choice is to interview our friends and family on tape and ask them what they remember about Charlotte and me as a couple.

Outcome

It's now been a year since Arthur answered the six questions, and here is what he tells us:

"I am glad that the idea about making tapes came to me when it did because Charlotte couldn't share those kinds of things with me now. The tapes where we tell each other how we feel about our years together are my favorite. I still don't know what it will be like when she can't recognize me anymore. My hope is that these tapes help me remember the best when I'm dealing with the worst."

Observations

Arthur used the questions to capture something dear to him—memories of his marriage to Charlotte. He was prompted to do that because time was running out. Even if you don't feel as if time is running out, we hope his story will inspire you to take action sooner rather than later.

No Dice

Rhonda and Jack are in their fifties. They have two grown children. Jack is a businessman. He is also a gambler whose wife is thinking about leaving him. As you follow Rhonda's account of events below, you will see how her answers to the basic questions moved her to make one last-ditch attempt to stay in the marriage and gave her a practical way to protect herself in case things didn't work out. This account is a good example of how to move forward effectively and with goodwill even when your partner cannot or will not cooperate.

Here is Rhonda's story:

"At the urging of both my children, I recently arranged a private meeting with our accountant. When I left the accountant's office, I was very upset. He had made it perfectly clear to me that unless things changed, my financial future looked grim. He said even though Jack earns a six-figure income, I probably wouldn't have enough money to pay for my basic necessities in a few years. Now, I realize that I cannot afford to stay in this marriage.

"My checks are bouncing, there's a huge pile of unpaid bills on my desk, 'questionable' charges are showing up on my credit-card statement, and I'm afraid to answer the phone because bill collectors are hounding me. This is nothing new. It's been that way off and on for years.

"Except for the few times Jack would 'hit it big' and pay off all our debts, we have always lived hand to mouth. I used to have to hide the money we needed for living expenses, knowing that the kids might go without food and clothing if I didn't. I even made regular runs by the pawn shop looking for things that were 'missing' from home.

"In the past, when I talked to Jack about his gambling, he'd beg, plead for another chance, and yet gamble again. He always promised he'd stop. And it was always a lie.

"I've read a lot about gambling. I've consulted with therapists, and I've gone to twelve-step support groups. Nothing I do makes any difference at all. I am too tired and too worried to keep on like this.

"I have stayed married to Jack this long because I thought that was best for the children. But the kids are grown, and if I continue on with Jack, I'll end up a penniless old lady who can barely pay for her own food. This isn't a question of whether or not I love him—I probably do. But Jack's gambling has destroyed too much of our lives. If I stay, things will only get worse."

Although Rhonda believed she had no other choice but to leave her marriage, she decided to use her answers to the basic questions to sort out her feelings and, in a last ditch effort, to look again at her options.

Her written responses to the questions follow:

Question 1: What are my negative feelings?

Livid at Jack for doing this to me again, *frustrated* that I can't change a damn thing about Jack's gambling, a bit *sad* about leaving my marriage, *worried* I might not stick to my guns about leaving Jack, *anxious* about my future, *angry* about all the financial worries I've had to deal with all these years.

Question 2: What's the fairest way to describe the problem?

Jack is a gambler. ~~He has not or cannot stop gambling. Either way,~~ his behavior puts my financial future at risk. Security is a major issue to me. I am getting older, and I believe that it would be best for me to leave our marriage now, while I am still employable. I wish there were some other solution. I do not think there is.

Question 3: Why do I want to work things out?

~~It breaks my heart to have to walk away from our marriage. I wish there was some other solution.~~ When he isn't gambling, we enjoy each other's company, and that is when being married to Jack is good.

Question 4: How would I like things between us to be?

I would like us to be able to plan for a secure future together, which means no more gambling. Specifically, I would like Jack to:

1. Attend Gamblers Anonymous (GA) meetings every evening for a while and then as many times a week as his sponsor suggests.
2. Get a GA sponsor.
3. Ask his sponsor to get in touch with me and serve as a person who can reassure me that he is making progress in the program.
4. Turn the checkbooks, credit cards, and all money management over to me.

Question 5: How can I actually get that?

I can ask our accountant to meet with me and help me come up with a financial plan to pay off Jack's debt. I can also ask him what must be done to make me the one who is in control of our money. Then I can lay down the law to Jack and tell him he has one year to prove that he can stop gambling. I can tell him that, as he knows, I do not believe in divorce and I have never before threatened to leave him. But if he gambles again, I will file for divorce. If I say this, I will mean it. And what I can also tell him is that he has to get help by doing the four things above or get a lawyer. Jack has no other choice. To help me get through this, I can ask both the children and our accountant to be there with me when I say all this to Jack.

Question 6: And if that doesn't work, what else can I do?

If he gambles again, divorce him. I can sell the house and use the profits to support myself while I get my real-estate license so I can go back to work.

Outcome

Within a few months, Rhonda told us:

"I had the kids and our accountant come over to the house, and we all sat down and had a talk with Jack. It was uncomfortable, but it was long overdue. Jack tried to rationalize a lot of things, but I held firm, and he finally agreed to everything I asked for. It turned out that our debt was even larger than I had known.

"We sold our home, used most of the money to pay off Jack's debt, and moved into a small apartment near Jack's office. I put the rest of the money from the sale of our house into a savings account in my name to use if Jack gambled again. That money was earmarked to help me start over on my own.

"Jack went to GA meetings three times a week. I handled our money. His paychecks got deposited automatically, and he couldn't write checks or with-draw funds from any of our accounts. We notified the bank of all this.

"In some ways, I felt like I was living with an irresponsible child. In other ways, it was like getting my husband back. Unfortunately, Jack started gam-bling again. I followed through with my back-up plan, and we got a divorce. But at least I left our marriage knowing I'd done everything I could.

"Even though this might sound like an unhappy ending, that's only partly true. For the first time in my life, I'm taking care of myself. I like that. I do spend time with Jack at the kids' homes, and we sometimes go out for dinner.

It's easier to enjoy him now that I don't have to worry about keeping a roof over my head. I wish this had turned out differently. But if I'd stayed, I'd be angry, bitter, and broke. As things stand now, I can relax around Jack and enjoy the time we spend together."

Observations

During nearly all the years of her marriage, Rhonda had been so busy trying to raise her children and run a household despite the chaos and fear that Jack's gambling produced that she hadn't addressed her need for financial security. It took her children's insistence that she meet privately with her accountant to bring that to her attention.

The basic questions in this case helped Rhonda get very clear about her needs and limits. And after she had done her best to salvage her marriage, she was able to walk away without guilt, hostility, regrets, or bitterness—and maintain some kind of positive relationship with Jack.

Only a Stone Should Live Alone

Following the death of a spouse, getting on with life is a struggle for many. Here you will see how one woman used the questions to move beyond the belief that her commitment to the past prohibited her from enjoying the present.

Iris is a woman in her mid-sixties whose husband, Marvin, died unexpectedly two years ago. Since then, she has continued to talk to him on a regular basis, and she feels that somehow he's watching over her.

She described her dilemma as follows:

"I realize that I have to go on without Marvin. I know it may sound crazy, but talking to him every night before I go to sleep helps me feel less lonely. And you know what? I'd rather do that than bother making conversation with a living man. After all the wonderful things Marvin did for me, enjoying myself with or even talking to another man seems a betrayal of his memory. Besides, it's a near miracle to find love once, much less twice. And it seems that men my age are all looking for younger women, so I might as well save myself the trouble and heartache.

"I know your questions are for people who want to work things out in their marriages. Obviously, Marvin isn't here in the flesh for me to work things out with him. But just out of curiosity, I'd like to answer the questions anyway."

This is what Iris wrote down in response to the questions:

Question 1: What are my negative feelings?

Lonely. Uneasy at the idea of meeting another man. *Afraid* my sixty-four–year-old body couldn't attract a man or hold his interest for long anyway.

Question 2: What's the fairest way to describe the problem?

Marvin died two years ago. The problem is that I feel as if I'm the one who's stopped living. The world is so full of things best enjoyed with a partner that I find myself wishing for the company of another man, but then I feel so disloyal to Marvin.

Question 3: Why do I want to work things out?

Because I'd like to be able to enjoy male companionship without feeling guilty.

Question 4: How would I like things between us to be?

I'd like to feel that even if I start seeing other men, Marvin will keep watching over me. I'd really like him to let me know that he'd be okay with me meeting another man.

Question 5: How can I actually get that?

I suppose I could discuss this with Marvin and see what he has to say.

Question 6: And if that doesn't work, what else can I do?

Think about joining a bereavement group.

Outcome

"My answers to the questions showed me that I'd been avoiding telling Marvin how I really felt. I finally decided it was time for us to have an honest discussion. I said, 'Marvin, I love you with all my heart, and I will feel that love until

I die. But I'm lonely, and I'm thinking about dating, maybe even remarrying someday. I don't know how you'd feel about that or whether it's the right thing to do. Remember how we always agreed that 'only a stone should live alone?' I think that if you would continue watching over me, I might be willing to date and someday even remarry.'

"After that, I said if it was okay with him for me to begin socializing again to give me a sign. Within a week, Marvin's sister phoned and said, 'Iris, it's been two years since Marvin's been gone and I know a gentleman I'd like to introduce you to. I know Marvin would not want you to live alone for the rest of your life. So what do you say?'

"I grinned and said, 'All signs point to yes.'"

Observations

In this story, Iris's curiosity about the questions and her willingness to answer them honestly helped her find a way to resolve her conflict about moving on without Marvin. Some would say her way of working through her problem was most creative. Others might say Marvin answered Iris in a loving manner.

Either way, we think this is another good example of how making a truthful effort to respond to the questions can help you get unstuck and start moving forward.

THOUGHTS TO TAKE WITH YOU

To connect with goodwill through divorce, loss, and life after that here's what can help:

- Consider taking "unwedding vows" to help your children adjust.
- Make the most of your relationship now (do this even if you don't feel as if time is running out).
- Be willing to move through the grieving process in order to put the past in perspective without letting go of it.

16

Now What?

It's your turn

Thank you for reading our book. We hope you have gotten as much out of your encounters with the people you've just heard from as we have. Something about the collective power of their personal stories continues to feed our imaginations and pop new approaches into our minds when we least expect it. We also hope that their successes will leave you feeling less alone and more optimistic, as they did for us, knowing that it really is possible to alter the tone and improve the outcome of your own disputes.

Beyond making life a little easier and perhaps more enjoyable for you and your partner, we have found that the value of asking and answering the basic questions boils down to this: even when you are feeling attacked, blamed, angry, or fearful, asking those questions moves you steadily beyond the natural tendency to dwell on who's right and who's wrong so you can concentrate on thinking about what you can do to change things for the better.

It seems to us that a woman who read an early draft of this book put it best:

"At first, I wanted to read your book because I thought it would show me how to win an argument with my husband. I zoomed in on the first four words in the title: 'I'm Right. You're Wrong.' But I quickly realized that the most helpful words in the title (at least for me) were the last two: 'Now What?' Those two words put the emphasis where it belongs: on paying more attention to *what* you can do to fix things and a whole lot less on *who* caused the problem in the first place. That made a major shift in my approach to an argument. Now, when we argue, I can actually get somewhere."

We hope that, from its title on, this book shifts your way of thinking about your own couples' conflicts. And most of all, we hope that it leaves you feeling enthused about going out into the world with a commitment to take the high road and use the six basic questions to guide you along the way.

Now What?

Now it's *your* turn to ask the questions.

Appendix

To address your own "I'm Right/You're Wrong"
couples' conflicts, use this worksheet as a guide

Question 1:	Answer:	Distracting Thoughts and Worries:
What are my negative feelings? • Pay attention to all your negative feelings. • Toward whom? • Eliminate **should/ shouldn't.** • Replace or remove blaming words. • Get rid of negative labels.		

Question 2:	Answer:	Distracting Thoughts and Worries:
What's the fairest way to describe the problem? • We are different. • No blaming, explaining, or guessing. • Remove phrases implying you're stuck. • What do we usually do?		

Question 3:	Answer:	Distracting Thoughts and Worries:
Why do I want to work things out? • Focus on positive feelings and/or practical reasons.		

Question 4:	Answer:	Distracting Thoughts and Worries:
How would I like things between us to be? • Specify your partner's realistic actions. • What would the perfect partner do? • Turn what you **don't** want into what you **do** want.		

Question 5:	Answer:	Distracting Thoughts and Worries:
How can I actually get that? • When, where, under what circumstances? • Specify your actions. • Brainstorm if you're stuck. • Keep your goal in mind. • Rehearse blame-free statement. • Handle worries. • Rehearse again.		

Question 6:	Answer:	Distracting Thoughts and Worries:
And if that doesn't work, what else can I do? • When, where, under what circumstances? • Keep your goal in mind. • Specify your actions. • Rehearse blame-free statement. • Handle worries. • Rehearse again.		

Index

About the Authors

JacLynn Morris, M.Ed., is a writer, child-abuse prevention advocate, and public speaker. A graduate of Boston University with a master's degree in counseling, her thirty-year career has included a wide range of positions from therapist to mayoral press secretary to marketing director for a chain of theme parks. As a therapist, she worked with families in crisis, parents of children with hemophilia, and adult survivors of child abuse. Articles she has written have appeared in magazines including *Moment* magazine, *Writing from the Heart*, and *Personal Journaling*. JacLynn lives in Atlanta with her husband of twenty-five years, Bruce H. Morris, a respected criminal defense attorney. They have two grown children, both of whom are pursuing acting careers.

Paul L. Fair, Ph.D., a graduate of Boston University, is a licensed clinical psychologist in private practice specializing in anxiety, anger, and stress disorders, individual and couples psychotherapy, biofeedback, and divorce coaching. Additionally, he consults with, produces, and oversees the development of stress reduction products and programs for Stressless, Inc. Dr. Fair lives in Atlanta with his wife, Virginia, a conference logistics professional. They have a grown daughter who is pursuing a career in art education and pottery.

Morris and Fair have coauthored two books: *From Me to You: The reluctant writer's guide to powerful, personal messages* and *I'm Right. You're Wrong. Now What?*

You can learn more about their work, read an interview, check upcoming appearances and book signings, and correspond with them at: www.imrightyourewrong.com.